Blessings,
Jo Anne
(Vannoy)
Goetz

This is a beautiful story, and I clearly heard Jo Anne's voice reading it to me. Leigh Somerville McMillan has captured her point of view, her voice, her faith.

Mark Rabil, Attorney for Darryl Hunt

Leigh Somerville McMillan gives us an intimate portrait of Jo Anne Goetz and her friendship with a man wrongly accused of murder – a story of race, justice and redemption.

Phoebe Zerwick, State Editor
The Winston-Salem Journal

It is a rare moment in life when people come together, not only to bring out the best in each other, but the best in humanity. Jo Anne Goetz is one of those rare treasures who not only stops and listens, but who knows the truth.

Helice "Sparky" Bridges, Founder & President
Difference Makers International and author of
"Who I Am Makes a Difference"

What a chilling story of love, compassion, longsuffering, courage, deliverance and freedom. Jo Anne Goetz captures the innocence of the human spirit. This is a powerful book

Dwight Lewis, Associate Athletic Director
Student-Athlete Services, Wake Forest University

Jo Anne Goetz is among a vanishing breed of teachers -- those whose love and care for their students extends far beyond the classroom.

Angelia J. Fryer, Ed.D.
Asst. Superintendent for Middle School
Administration

A courageous inspiration of what is possible when you believe with absolute certainty that it is our place (as human beings) to maintain faith while sharing love and kindness with others.

Keith Froehling, International Inspirational Speaker

It was hard to stop reading this book, which says quite a bit about its flow and its interest. Ms. McMillan does a very good job with a story that, from a personal and intuitive point of view, leads the reader to the fallacy of the verdict.

Paul Bledsoe, President
Bledsoe Advertising/Productions

Every experienced teacher knows kids can spot sincerity in a heartbeat; so it was for Jo Anne Goetz and Darryl Hunt. This book is an accurate account of a city which still grapples with racial prejudice and offers the lesson that the smallest deed is worth doing if it makes a difference in a child's life. The book is not only a story about the difficult political choices Goetz made but is also filled with many teaching tips.

Sammie Goodwin ATR-BC NCC LPC
Middle School Academy

LONG TIME COMING

My Life and the Darryl Hunt Lesson

as told by
Jo Anne North Goetz

and written by
Leigh Somerville McMillan

Bloomington, IN Milton Keynes, UK

authorHOUSE®

AuthorHouse™
1663 Liberty Drive, Suite 200
Bloomington, IN 47403
www.authorhouse.com
Phone: 1-800-839-8640

AuthorHouse™ UK Ltd.
500 Avebury Boulevard
Central Milton Keynes, MK9 2BE
www.authorhouse.co.uk
Phone: 08001974150

First published by AuthorHouse 3/27/2007
ISBN: 978-1-4343-0170-3 (sc)

Library of Congress Control Number: 2007901854

Printed in the United States of America
Bloomington, Indiana

This book is printed on acid-free paper.

Illustration and Cover Design by Jeremy Owens

This book is dedicated to

Darryl Hunt

and

Anthony Burnett, Barry Sales and my other students
at Mebane Elementary School

and

Rita Taylor, my sister who believed in me
and in Darryl's innocence

"Instruction begins when you, the teacher, learn from the learner; put yourself in his place so that you may understand . . . what he learns and the way he understands it."

Soren Kierkegaard

LONG TIME COMING

My Life and the Darryl Hunt Lesson

I saw beyond the cornrows, sticking up
like angry spikes on his head.

CHAPTER ONE

When a teacher meets a student for the first time, she has no idea what effect that child may have on her life. Some hold a place in her heart for a year and then move on to make room for the next class. A few never lose their special role in the learning experience.

Darryl Hunt was one of those students who not only stayed in my heart, but became one of my greatest teachers. I learned from him a lesson much more important than the reading, writing and arithmetic I taught him.

I learned forgiveness.

The lesson began when I was 40 years old. Raised in a small community in the Appalachian Mountains, I became the first in the history of my family and my small high school to receive a college education. When I met Darryl Hunt, I had taught for 19 years in the public school system in the rural south and thought I was a pretty good judge of character.

As I looked at the young black man who sat across from me in the Forsyth County Jail in the fall of 1984, I knew I would go to my grave believing that Darryl Eugene Hunt was an innocent man – regardless of how many people placed their hands on the Bible and swore otherwise.

I knew as well as I knew that the sun rises every morning and sets every night that Darryl Hunt did not rape, sodomize and stab Deborah Sykes 16 times. Stabbed her to death.

I saw beyond the cornrows sticking up like angry spikes on his head. Beyond the 19-year-old accused of murder, I saw the round-faced little boy I had taught in the sixth grade at Mebane Elementary School.

Standing on tiptoe to hug Darryl in the airless, windowless visiting room at the jail in downtown Winston-Salem, I could still feel the scrawny little shoulders I had embraced for the last time in 1976.

When I looked at the hands gripping each other in his lap – hands that appeared big enough to wrap themselves around a basketball with plenty of room to spare -- I could still see them on the final day of school. Clutching like a hard-earned and well-deserved prize my picture and the poem I had written for him.

I still saw the boy who turned to wave good-bye with a smile that always lit up the world around him.

During my first jailhouse visit with Darryl on the Thursday before Thanksgiving 1984, I did not see a man arrested for murder two months before. Instead, I saw the 12-year-old child who stood up for me with the class bully, and I knew it was time to return the favor.

Little Nathan had been the kind of child who was always itching for a fight. Look at him the wrong way, and he balled up his fists. Life just wasn't fair, in Nathan's opinion.

I had told the children to line up to go to the nurse to get their eyes checked. I had given the girls their health cards and was working my way down the line of boys. When I gave Nathan his, he threw it on the floor.

"I'm not taking it," he growled. "You gave them to the girls first."

While I tried to figure out the best way to handle Nathan, Darryl very quietly walked over to him and said, "Pick up your card."

Nathan looked at him, and Darryl stared back and repeated, "Pick up your card. The girls always go first. That's the rule."

Nathan picked up his card.

From that day on, Darryl was my protector. I never saw him fight, and he was quick to stop one if he could.

Now, seven years later, he had been arrested, charged with first-degree murder and awaited a jury trial that could potentially lead to the death penalty. As soon as the image of Darryl strapped in the electric chair crossed my mind, I shut it out.

In the deepest place in my heart, I believed that Darryl had not murdered and trusted that he would not be convicted of that crime.

It could not happen.

I had read the article about the Sykes murder in the local paper. "Newswoman is stabbed to death," screamed the headlines of *The Winston-Salem Journal* on August 11, 1984.

The story reported that 26-year-old Deborah Brotherton Sykes, of Mooresville, had been stabbed to death during her two-block walk to work at *The Sentinel,* the *Journal's* afternoon paper. Her body, described as 5 feet 10 inches tall and weighing 150 pounds, was found partially clad on a grassy slope off West End Boulevard. The crime scene lay across the street from Crystal Towers, a high-rise apartment building for senior citizens.

I knew the area well. I had driven by it many times and had seen the empty beer cans and wine bottles that littered the hillside.

I refused to let my mind dwell on what had happened there to the fresh-faced young woman, walking to work without a care in the world.

The article reported that police were looking for two unidentified black men, 20 to 25 years old, 6 feet to 6 feet 3 inches tall, medium build and wearing dark clothing.

In interviews, people who knew Ms. Sykes as a strong, physically active woman, had said they didn't think one average-sized man could have overpowered her.

The reporter wrote that Ms. Sykes had begun her job as a copy editor at *The Sentinel* about a month before, and that she and her husband, John Douglas Sykes, Jr., had been living with his parents while looking for a house in Winston-Salem.

She left her in-laws' house in Mooresville at 5 a.m., and, about an hour later, parked her pale blue Opal Kadett on West End Boulevard, just north of Sixth Street. She began her usual walk to work.

Witnesses told police they saw her being forced to an area about 150 feet from her car. Her body was found lying just beyond a 4-foot tall wall of wooden posts.

The article reported that police searched for more than two hours before her body was found. After the police arrived, people working in the area realized that what they had thought was a pile of clothes was a body.

Lt. Jerry Raker of the Winston-Salem Police Department was quoted as saying that at least four witnesses saw Ms. Sykes before the attack.

When I read, "According to Raker, the witnesses saw one or two black men," I stopped and read the sentence again. They must not be very credible witnesses if they didn't know if there was one black man or two black men, I thought.

Whoever had killed her – one man or two men -- had stripped off her slacks. I read that an autopsy was being done to find evidence of rape.

A member of my church, Fred Flagler, the newspaper's managing editor, was interviewed for the story. He said that when Ms. Sykes was late for work, her supervisors had assumed her car had broken down. One of her co-workers found the blue Opal a few hours later. Her husband identified it, and they called the police.

Deborah Sykes' body was found between 1:45 and 2 p.m. It had lain in the August sun for eight hours.

That night, I watched as the local television station showed footage of the abandoned Opal and the stretcher being wheeled to the ambulance.

People in Winston-Salem debated the case at work, at church, on the street. The thought of murder was terrifying enough, but the thought of a black man – or two black men – raping and stabbing a white woman added the ugly racial demon to the picture. I felt as though I were living Harper Lee's *To Kill a Mockingbird*.

Men anguished over the idea that it could have been their mother, their wife, their sister, their daughter out there on that hill. Women feared that it could have been them.

*"I'm afraid Darryl's running with a bad
crowd, Ms. North," Anthony said.*

CHAPTER TWO

When I picked up the *Journal* on September 15, 1984,
I scanned the front page quickly. Classes had started
again, and I was in a hurry to get to my teaching job
at Philo Middle School.

The early morning sun streamed through the kitchen window
of the house Mother and I had shared since we both divorced.
Outside, the dogwood leaves had just begun to show a hint of
red, and chrysanthemums were covered with yellow and orange
buds.

Mother had fixed toast and poured my orange juice, and I sat
at the kitchen bar, enjoying my last sip of coffee.

As I looked at the article above the fold on the front page,
it took me a minute or two to focus on the picture. I read the
headline, "Man already in jail is charged in Sykes murder."

When I did turn my attention to the picture, I didn't recognize
the young man in cornrows. In fact, I was surprised. The earlier
article hadn't included cornrows in the description of the hunted
man – or men.

Like everybody else who read the paper that morning, I felt
a sense of relief that the police had arrested the killer. That this
brutal madman was off the streets.

By the second sentence, that feeling of relief had turned a sharp corner.

I read, "Darryl Eugene Hunt of 760 N. Patterson Ave. was charged with first-degree murder and is being held without bond in the Forsyth County Jail."

I dropped the paper and leaped off the barstool.

"You're not going to believe this," I called out to my mother. "They've arrested my Darryl."

Mother moved over to the bar, and I read the first few sentences out loud. I looked at the picture again. Staring back at me, Darryl's familiar almond-shaped eyes looked more like a scared animal than the gentle child of my memory. A scared animal caught in a trap.

No way, I said to myself. There's no way Darryl Hunt could have murdered anybody.

Then I remembered a conversation I had had a couple weeks earlier with Anthony Burnett.

Anthony was a classmate of Darryl's in my group of sixth graders at Mebane and, without a doubt, the smartest one in the class. I followed his progress after he left me, and when he graduated from Parkland High School, I got him a summer job washing dishes during Governor's School at Salem College.

The Governor's School of North Carolina was started in 1963 -- the first of its kind in the nation -- as a six-week summer residential program for intellectually gifted high school students. Funded by the General Assembly of North Carolina, it is free to all students and offers study in academics and the arts.

As the athletic director at the Governor's School, I often ran into Anthony during my days on campus. Any time I saw him, I encouraged him to fill out an application for the fall semester at Winston-Salem State University.

I figured if I could go to college, Anthony certainly could.

I was the first one in my family and one of the first two graduates of Fleetwood High School to go to college. During

7

the first half of this century, getting a college education was not a priority in Ashe County, North Carolina.

I dreamed about going away to school but never thought it would be possible. In fact, when I was preparing to leave for Appalachian State Teachers College in 1952, I overheard a neighbor say, "If Fred Vannoy's girl can go to college, anybody can." [1]

Everyone in Oval knew Daddy's story.

He loved to hunt, and one day in the third grade, he had stayed home from school to spend some time in the woods. As he passed by the schoolhouse, he saw his teacher walk out the front door.

Daddy was an excellent shot and decided to use the bricks holding up the steps as a target. Very carefully, he took aim and shot one out, causing the step to collapse and spilling the teacher out into the yard. Daddy never went back to school.

Since he never learned to read or write well, he supported his family with a meager income made by doing manual labor. He farmed, drove a truck, worked as a carpenter. My mother stayed at home until their four children were in school and then found a job as a saleslady at Smithey's Department Store in West Jefferson.

If I could rise above my own family's lack of education, I believed Anthony could, too. After much prodding, I succeeded in convincing him to take the Scholastic Aptitude Test. He studied all summer and, as I predicted, he aced the exam.

His next challenge was much harder for a poor boy from the projects to overcome – paying the college tuition.

With the idea of getting Anthony a wrestling scholarship and a grant to pay any remaining expenses, I drove over to WSSU to talk to the basketball coach, Clarence "Big House" Gaines. Big House and I had become friends during the years that I had taken

---

[1] Both my sisters, Peggy Hawkins and Rita Taylor, obtained college degrees and enjoyed careers as teachers.

the boys from Governor's School to his campus to use the weight-lifting equipment, and I hoped he could help Anthony.

Just as I had suspected, he was able to help, and Anthony registered for classes.

At the end of summer, Governor's School ended, and I went back to teaching sixth grade. Each time I thought about Anthony Burnett in college, I felt warm all over.

That feeling came to an abrupt end one day when I was at Salem picking up a book I had left in my office.

I ran into Anthony's cafeteria supervisor.

"Isn't it wonderful that Anthony Burnett is in college," I said.

"No, he isn't. He's right in the kitchen washing dishes."

"What in the world happened?"

"His mama needed his support at home.[2] She thinks he needs to keep his steady job here at Salem."

My warm feeling of success was replaced by a cold failure I had never known before.

The next time I ran into Anthony at Salem, he had been promoted to the painting crew.

"What's this I hear about you not going to college?" I asked.

"I'm sorry, Ms. North. Maybe one day."

Each time I had seen him, I had heard that same refrain, "Maybe one day."

As we stood talking the last day I ran into him, he seemed anxious to divert my attention away from himself to Darryl.

"Did you hear that Darryl Hunt is back from California?" he asked as soon as he saw me.

I told him I hadn't but that I wasn't surprised. Southern roots run deeper than most.

"Remember that time you caught us with all those silver dollars?" Anthony asked. "Darryl and me were exploring all over his grandfather's house, and we found jars and jars of coins up

---

[2] Anthony Burnett is still his mother's primary caregiver.

in the attic. We came to school with our pockets filled with all that money and you caught us and told us we had to take it back. We were fixing to go bowling or something after school and you nabbed us."

"I also remember something about you getting Darryl in trouble with the woman he mowed grass for," I prompted him.

"Yes, ma'am. She used to leave her garage door open so after he finished his work around the yard, he could go in and get the money she owed him out of her change jar. One day after school, Darryl and me wanted to buy ourselves some ice cream, but we didn't have no money, so we went over to the garage and emptied out that change jar. I went with him the next time he was supposed to mow the grass, and the garage door was locked and he couldn't get in. We waited around for the lady and when she finally came home, Darryl asked her why the door was locked. 'Somebody came in and stole all my money,' she said, 'and I don't know who that little boy you have with you is, but don't you bring him around here no more.'"

"What did Darryl do then?"

"We felt mighty bad about taking that lady's money, so the next day after school, we went over and mowed her yard and pulled all her weeds, and when she tried to pay us, we wouldn't take her money - - - seeing as how we'd already taken it before."

Anthony and I laughed at our shared memories, but then a cloud seemed to pass over his face.

"Darryl's not looking too good these days, Ms. North," Anthony said seriously. "He came over the other day, and we sat up on the hill behind my house and talked a little and shot tin cans with an old BB gun. He looked pretty bad. Eyes all bloodshot and clothes looking like he'd slept in them. I think he's hanging around with a bad crowd."

"You tell him to come see me," I said.

But Darryl hadn't come to see me. And a couple of weeks later, he was arrested for murder.

As I read about his arrest, I knew that the only way Darryl Hunt could have done something that violent would have been if he had been using drugs. The only thing Anthony had been worried about was his heavy drinking.

I looked at the picture again. The cornrows have to go, I thought, convinced that those glaring symbols of life on the streets would damn him as soon as the jury saw them.

He had been charged with first-degree murder the day before and was being held without bond in the Forsyth County Jail.

The full import of what Anthony had said about the bad company Darryl was keeping sank in the further I read.

Eight days before Deborah Sykes was killed, Darryl had been sentenced to six months in jail for trespassing and damaging personal property. He had appealed the sentence and was freed on $300 bond.

But, at the time he was charged with the Sykes murder, Darryl had been in jail again, awaiting trial on one count of taking indecent liberties with a minor – his 14-year-old girlfriend. His bond had been set at $25,000.

Maj. Joseph E. Masten, acting chief of the Winston-Salem Police Department, was quoted in the article as saying that only one person had been charged with the murder, but that another man might be involved. "Thus far our investigation doesn't support that," he had said.

I read that a witness had seen a man "holding Ms. Sykes around the head and neck in an assaultive manner."

My heart stopped when I read that the witness, "a longtime member of the community with no criminal history, identified that man as Hunt from a photographic lineup this week. The witness spoke to police on the day of the murder but could provide only a description of the killer, not a name. The turning point in the case came last week, Masten said, but he declined to elaborate."

Police had drawn a warrant to take hair, blood and saliva samples from Hunt in jail to match it with samples taken from Ms. Sykes' body. As I read those words, my mouth felt as dry as a cotton field that hasn't seen rain in months.

They had also drawn a search warrant for Mattie Mitchell's apartment on Patterson Ave., where Darryl was living with her son, Sammy Lee Mitchell. The article reported that police were looking for a black T-shirt and dark or black pants, fitting the description that witnesses had given of what the men were wearing. They were also looking for a knife with a 5-inch blade or shorter, matching the wounds inflicted on the body.

The police had found what they were looking for at Ms. Mitchell's apartment -- a black T-shirt and a pocketknife with a broken tip.

My hands shook as I read that Darryl had been brought handcuffed to the warrants office to have the warrant served on him. His face "betrayed no emotion as the charge was read to him," the reporter wrote.

I had seen that face more than once in the sixth grade. I knew what Darryl had done that day in the warrants office. He had gone into the protective shell children of the projects build for themselves. A safe place where they can watch the horror around them but not be hurt.

A reward of $12,000 had been offered for information on the murder. Douglas Sykes was quoted as saying he felt "a big relief" about the arrest.

My hands shook as I laid the paper down.

I knew Darryl had no family. No advocates. I knew he needed my help.

The first person I called was District Attorney Don Tisdale. He and I bowled in the same league.

"Don," I said, "this is Jo Anne North. I saw the article about Darryl Hunt. Darryl was my student, and I'm sure you've got the wrong person. This young man is not capable of such a violent crime."

"I know, but I think he knows something about it," was Don's reply.

Encouraged by Don's comment and yet knowing Darryl would need as many advocates in his corner as he could get, I called Walter Marshall. I had taught his son, Malcolm and knew Walter was involved with the NAACP.

When he answered the phone, I identified myself and said, "Mr. Marshall, did you see Darryl Hunt's picture in the paper today?"

He had not.

I repeated my conversation with Tisdale. "I taught Darryl, and I am convinced he did not kill Deborah Sykes. I think this is something you and the NAACP need to get involved with."

He said he was aware of how well I knew my students and told me that he'd look into it.

I went on to school, hoping I had helped in some small way by getting people involved – people who could make a difference.

I didn't make any plans to go visit Darryl. I expected to hear within days that he had been released.

Darryl looked at me like a drowning man who sees a rotten board floating in rough seas. He's not sure it can save him, but he grabs it and holds on for dear life.

CHAPTER THREE

After a couple of months had passed, and Darryl was still behind bars, I knew I needed to go see him.

I wasn't sure that I would be allowed to visit, but I knew one person at the jail who could help me get in – Sheriff's Deputy Tommy Andrews. Tommy's wife, Gwen, and I worked together. I had helped her get her first job in the school system and, at the time of Darryl's arrest, she was my paraprofessional at Philo.

I took her aside one day after school.

"Gwen, will you ask Tommy if he can arrange for me to see Darryl?"

She said she would. The next day she came back and said that Tommy had been able to get my name on Darryl's visiting list, and that I could visit as long as I came during the shift on which he was the supervisor.

Within a week, I was on my way to see Darryl Hunt.

I drove downtown to the Forsyth County Jail in early afternoon on the Thursday before Thanksgiving, feeling as though I was on a journey to a foreign land. Alone.

The day was cold, and I was surprised to see a man sitting outside on the front steps. As I got closer, I realized that I was looking at Sammy Mitchell, Darryl's running buddy, the other half of the local "Blues Brothers." I suspected that he was the "bad company" Anthony had talked about.

I walked up the steps very slowly.

"Good morning," I said and smiled. "How are you?"

Sammy just nodded. He didn't know who I was, but I had seen his picture in the paper more than once.

I walked into the lobby, announced at the desk I was there to see Deputy Andrews and was told to find a seat and wait. I sat, hunkered down in my heavy coat, clutched my purse in my lap and looked out of the corner of my eyes at the other people waiting with me.

Most of the other visitors were women and much younger than my 50 years. Many were holding babies or trying unsuccessfully to control toddlers. Few were white.

I felt surrounded and realized I was probably feeling what Darryl had as one of only eight blacks in my classroom. How he and other blacks felt many times in their lives.

The image of Darryl in the electric chair tried to force itself into my mind again, and I kept telling myself that he didn't do it. He's innocent. He won't be convicted. This will all be over soon.

I wondered if anybody else had come to see friends or family charged with murder. Trying not to stare, I looked around at the other faces but didn't see anybody who appeared to feel as nervous as I did. Most looked bored. Like they had sat in those same seats too often and wanted to get in and out as fast as possible.

About 10 minutes after I arrived, Tommy came into the lobby and led me over to the desk to sign in. My heart beat so hard and so fast that I was afraid it would jump out of my coat and on to the counter as I signed my name on the visitors list.

I was told to put my purse in a locker, and I walked over to the elevator with Tommy. He stepped aside for me to enter first and pushed the button to take us up to the floor where Darryl was being held.

The elevator door shut, and we were alone.

"Ms. North, why are you so sure Darryl Hunt is innocent?" Tommy asked.

"Because he has a peaceful heart," I said. "It's that simple."

"When did you teach him?"

"Sixth grade."

I could see the wheels turning in Tommy's head and knew that those same wheels would turn whenever I spoke in Darryl's defense. I suspected that Tommy was thinking what everyone would think – maybe he's changed in seven years.

Tommy didn't voice any opinion.

"What was he like?" he asked.

"Quiet. Helpful. He never fought and was always the one to stop a fight. I know him, Tommy. I know he didn't kill Deborah Sykes."

Tommy just nodded.

As we stepped off the elevator and walked down the long hall to the visiting room, I could feel the sweat beading on my forehead. My body was hot under my winter coat.

Tommy opened the door to a small room not much bigger than my walk-in bedroom closet, and I went in and sat down on one of the two straight-backed wooden chairs. Tommy left to go get Darryl.

As I sat alone, I could hear my pulse in my ears. Everything else was quiet.

Finally, I heard footsteps. The door opened, and there stood Darryl Hunt. Tommy ushered him in and then stood outside the door so he could watch and yet offer us some privacy.

I rose to my feet, and my knees almost buckled under me. Darryl caught me in a hug that erased the seven years since we had last seen each other.

I stepped back and held him at arm's length.

"You've got to get rid of the cornrows," were the first words out of my mouth.

Darryl didn't say anything. He smiled and looked at me like he couldn't believe what he saw. I was his first personal visitor, he said, and he looked at me like a drowning man who sees a rotten board floating in rough seas. He's not sure it can hold him up, but he grabs it and holds on for dear life.

We sat down on the same side of the small table and inched our chairs as close as we could to each other. He hung his head and we sat in silence for a while.

Believing in his innocence, I had no need to talk about the crime, and I didn't want to talk about the injustice. Knowing my faith in him, words seemed unnecessary to Darryl, as well.

I knew we needed to talk about practicalities instead.

"Darryl Hunt, when I come to visit you, you look at me," I said in my best no-nonsense teacher's voice. "When we go to court, and you sit at that table and look down all the time, that jury is going to say, 'Look at him. He must be guilty. He won't even look up.' So, every time I come to visit you, you always look at me when we talk. Let's practice."

Darryl looked up and said, "Yes, ma'am, Ms. North."

"Was that Sammy Mitchell I saw sitting out front?"

"Yes, ma'am. Probably was."

"He's nothing but trouble, Darryl."

"Yes, ma'am, but his mama took me in when I didn't have nobody. He's all I've got."

I certainly couldn't argue with that.

What I knew about Darryl's past was a bare bones story.

He and his older brother, Willie, had been raised by their grandfather, William Stroud.

When he was 9 years old and in the third grade, Darryl had learned that Jean Hunt, the woman who had visited him on weekends, was his mother. One week later, she had been murdered.

He had never known his father.

During the summer after his sixth grade, when he was 12, his grandfather had died.

I had heard the story that Mr. Stroud hadn't trusted banks and that Darryl was the one who had known where he kept his money. After the funeral, Darryl retrieved $10,000 from his grandfather's attic, $5,000 from the trunk of his car and $4,000 buried in his backyard.

Mr. Stroud's brothers divided the money and went back to South Carolina, leaving Darryl and his brother Willie with their grandfather's sister, Ann Lee Johnson. She, too, died the next year.

At 16, Darryl dropped out of the ninth grade at South Park High School, and moved to Monterey, California, to live with his stepsister Juanita Johnson. I wasn't surprised by the news that Darryl had left school. I knew he had an average ability to learn and, when I'd heard that he had been placed in a school for the learning disabled, I became afraid he would become discouraged.

I also believed it wasn't my place to interfere in another teacher's decision and decided not to voice my objection to the placement.

Before he left Winston-Salem, Darryl visited Carl Russell, his grandfather's funeral director, and learned that Mr. Stroud had set up a $10,000 trust fund to which he would become entitled after his 18th birthday.

With that to look forward to, Darryl set out for California in 1980.

For six months, he took night classes at Monterey Adult School and then dropped out of school again to go to work. He was employed by a gardening service and then as a dishwasher at Rendezvous Bakery. His eight-hour shift at the bakery ended after the busses stopped running, and Darryl walked 17 miles home.

As soon as he turned 18, he headed back to Winston-Salem to collect his inheritance, rent an apartment and find a job. Working construction, Darryl began dating the boss's pregnant daughter, Rene, who moved in with him and accepted his financial and emotional support with the baby.

When Rene left, she took with her the baby girl Darryl had loved like his own daughter.

The only living family he had was his brother, Willie, who was serving time in jail.

As I sat in the jailhouse with Darryl Hunt, I could understand his words, "Sammy is all I've got."

I searched for something to talk about. Darryl was as quiet a man as he had been as a boy, and I felt he would have been content simply sitting with me. I was the one who wanted to fill the empty space with words – memories of Mebane.

CHAPTER FOUR

I was 40 years old and had been teaching for 19 years when I met Darryl Hunt in 1975. He was 12 years old and a student in my sixth grade class at Mebane Elementary School on the east side of Winston-Salem – the black side of town.

I had transferred to Mebane from the Methodist Children's Home three years earlier, when the decision was made to move the orphans and their teachers into the county school system. I had requested a teaching assignment close enough to the orphanage so that I could easily drive there and continue to coach basketball after classes were over for the day.

Basketball – any sports, for that matter – was my passion, and I refused to give it up.

My father loved athletics. I was the oldest of his four children and the only one who shared his interest in sports.

As a child, I was a natural athlete, and I think my father was proud to hear that I was always chosen first for the softball team. He loved to boast about my accomplishments as a high jumper and a runner.

When I enrolled at Appalachian State Teachers College, my plan was to major in physical education, but my work in the cafeteria and the library didn't leave me enough time to meet all the requirements for that degree. Instead, I graduated with a major in grammar grade education and minors in social studies and physical education.

Because my public school teaching job didn't give me the opportunity to pursue my passion for sports, I was determined to maintain my coaching position at the Children's Home. The fact that Mebane was within 10 miles of the orphanage gave me the time in my schedule to make the drive.

When I accepted the job there, friends who didn't realize the school was in Winston-Salem were puzzled.

"Why in the world are you driving all the way to Mebane?" they asked, confusing the school with Mebane, North Carolina, which was located more than an hour from Winston-Salem.

Mebane Elementary School was geographically close, but it was worlds away from anything in my prior teaching experience. That first year, in my class of 30 students, I taught my first four black children.

Mebane had been an all-black school before integration in 1969. When I arrived, the white students were there, but the school, itself, had not yet been brought up to the same standards considered acceptable in the formerly all-white schools.

The bricks in the two-story building on Vargrave Avenue looked old and tired, and the paint on the doors and windowsills had started flaking years ago. The students' and teachers' desks bore the scars of years and years of use and abuse.

I remember being warned by a teacher who had recently left her position there.

"I'm so sorry to hear you're going to Mebane," she said.

"Why?" I asked.

"It's a horrible place."

"What's so horrible about it?"

The woman hesitated a fraction of a second and then pulled me aside.

"There's a house of ill repute right across the street," she whispered. "There's people going in and coming out of there all the time."

She stopped to measure my reaction.

I hesitated as though I were weighing my options.

"Well, I'm not considering getting a second job," I said, pretending to be serious. "I think I'll have all I can handle with my teaching."

My friends were concerned about my safety in a predominantly black and run-down neighborhood. I thought about their warnings on my first day of school.

As I got out of my car, the first thing I saw was a group of men watching me from across the street. They whistled and made some remarks I couldn't hear but was sure weren't acceptable in polite society.

I threw back my shoulders, made my 5 foot 5 inches as tall as I could and marched up the sidewalk. "How y'all doin?" I waved and kept walking.

Six weeks later, I wondered if one of those men had run up the stairs and into my second-floor classroom.

I had taken my students to the school library and left my purse in the closet next to my desk. On our way back to class, a stranger dashed out of my room, and one of my students yelled, "Ms. North, he's got your pocketbook."

The thief got away before anybody could catch him.

The most painful part of the drama was that I suspected one of my students had helped hatch the plan. Somebody had to have told the thief when we'd be gone and where I kept my purse.

I felt betrayed by the students I had trusted, but intuitively I knew to keep those feelings to myself.

I sat the children down very calmly that day.

"Children, as you know, my pocketbook has been stolen," I said and waited while the flurry of voices died down. "I will appreciate your trying to help me find it. I don't want to have to go to all the trouble of getting a new driver's license and credit cards, so please ask your friends if they know anything about where mine are."

I didn't ask questions. I didn't accuse. I simply moved a locked file cabinet into the room and kept my purse there from that day on.

A few days later, a woman who lived near the school called and said she had found the contents of my purse scattered in her yard.

The boy I suspected of directing the robbery did a complete about-face. Anything I needed done, he did. Anything I wanted, he made sure I got. I felt as though I had passed some kind of test.

* * *

I faced another challenge that first year that took a little more engineering -- the open classroom.

Sharing a room with 60 students and one other teacher seemed to catapult me back to the 1940s in Oddie Cox's one-room schoolhouse in Ashe County.

During those years before integration, all the blacks in the county attended one school and every black child was taught by Oddie, a little old scrawny black man who inspired me to become a teacher.

In my opinion, Oddie Cox was the best teacher in the county. He cared about his students.

Behind the steering wheel of an old rusted blue van, he cruised the county, gathering up the black children and depositing them at school. Anyone driving along in the early dawn saw little clusters of black children huddled together after walking miles along dirt roads to meet Oddie's bus at the main road.

After he had them all collected – first graders through twelfth graders -- Oddie took out the tattered and torn textbooks handed down from the white schools, and he taught. Textbooks like *The Blueback Speller* came to life under the skillful teaching of Oddie Cox.

While my knowledge of his classroom was secondhand, I had the good fortune of hearing him preach several times. Oddie Cox was a well-educated man, a true orator who possessed a natural gift for teaching.

My open classroom in Winston-Salem in the 1970s was similar, but I wasn't Oddie Cox.

I withstood the constant noise and moving around as long as I could, but I had my own ideas of what worked and what didn't work. I had taught for 16 years, and I believed it was impossible for me to get to know 60 students well enough to make any kind of difference in their lives.

Finally, I took advantage of the fact that one of my neighbors was assistant school superintendent and called him on the phone one night when I was at my wit's end.

"Either you build a wall and split the room into two classes, or I'm going to have to find myself something else to do," I said. "I've had it."

A couple of days later, workmen converged on the school and built a wall. When the students arrived on Monday, they were divided into two classes. I could still hear the voices on the other side of the cork wall, but at least they weren't my responsibility.

* * *

Darryl Hunt was one of eight black students in my class of 30 children during my last year at Mebane.

What I saw when Darryl walked in my room the first day of school was a 12-year-old boy who had already given up.

His downcast eyes and slumped shoulders spoke volumes. "I'm here. I know I'm not much, but I'll try," his body language spoke loud and clear.

24

I had seen it before, but the difference with Darryl and some of the other children I had met was that he did try.

When Darryl Hunt entered my classroom in 1976, he walked into a new world -- a home environment he told me he looked forward to every day.

In the room Darryl and I shared, a long row of eight closet doors lined one wall. I had looked at those doors, had seen the perfect place to display student artwork and borrowed acrylic paint from the art teacher. On each of four of the doors, the children painted the same country scene as it changed during the four seasons. On the other set of four doors, they painted Disney characters.

At the back of the room, large windows looked out at the neighborhood I had been warned about. Rumor was that it could be as dangerous as the yellow jacket's nest that appeared every fall on the shelf outside one of the windows.

I created a curtain of green plants to hide the ugliness outside. The ugliness of peeling paint and trashy yards across the street. Every window ledge was covered with pots, and I found that 30 children breathing on the philodendron every day worked wonders.

My class loved the aloe vera best. The very thought that it had magical powers that could heal burns made them curious, and, if I didn't keep an eye on them, the plants mysteriously lost pieces overnight.

I opened the windows whenever the weather permitted. Quite often, the air was filled with the sweet aroma of tobacco being processed at the R. J. Reynolds Tobacco manufacturing plant. On those days when the air hung heavy with that familiar smell, the children inhaled deeply and pretended to get high.

When the windows were closed, we were enveloped by the scent of the green sawdust the janitor sprinkled on the old wood floors at night to keep down the dust. In the mornings, the sawdust transformed the floors into skating rinks even the most well-behaved children couldn't resist.

On the first day of school, Darryl Hunt took his seat in a wooden desk in the middle of that room.

I always seated my students in alphabetical order so I could remember their names, and they sat in that order until I had committed their names to memory. Then I shifted them each week. The children in the back came to the front, and everyone else moved back a seat.

That was just one of the ways I tried to create fairness in a world that my students were already experiencing as pretty unfair.

My desk sat at the front, across from a large slate blackboard. The children took turns carrying the erasers outside to bang them against the side of the building to get the chalk dust out, and it was a rare child who could resist banging them in somebody's face on the way out the door to make him sneeze.

Darryl was that rare child. A serious boy, he seemed to want nothing more than to please me in any way he could. I recognized early in the year that he wouldn't excel in his studies. He read on a third grade level the year he came to me.

But I saw that he could excel in other ways. He was a helper, and he did so many things that year to make my life easier, starting with protecting my car.

We teachers parked our cars behind the school in a lot that sloped steeply down towards the building. One day during a snowstorm, a vehicle slid down the hill and crashed into a wall, creating a great deal of excitement for the children.

But a bigger problem than slippery asphalt was the car battery thieves who did their business during the nights we held PTA meetings. On more than one night after the meetings, I walked out into the parking lot to find Darryl, standing in the dark, guarding my car.

Darryl's grandfather, William Stroud, wasn't a member of the PTA, but he never missed a parent/teacher conference.

Darryl and his brother Willie lived with the old man on Maryland Avenue, within walking distance of the school. When Mr. Stroud walked into my classroom to talk about how Darryl was doing in my class, I recognized a proud man. Proud of Darryl. And unlike many of the other children who dreaded the embarrassment of their parents meeting with their teacher, Darryl seemed to love the thought of Mr. Stroud and me together. I could see that he was as proud of his grandfather as Mr. Stroud was of him.

Mr. Stroud had gotten his GED so that he could be promoted to foreman of the streets division of the city maintenance department, and he told me he wanted his grandson to be educated, too. When he took his checks to the bank to be cashed, he took Darryl with him so that he could learn about money. And he cleaned him up and dressed him in his Sunday-go-to-meeting clothes and sat with him on a pew in the First Calvary Baptist Church so he could learn about God.

"How's Darryl doing?" the old man asked at every parent teacher conference, taking off his hat and holding it in his lap. A recent widower, he sat in front of me alone, spreading out in the chair as though he still felt the woman beside him. As though he were saving her seat in the world.

I watched as he fidgeted in his chair, eyes darting around the room, taking in the artwork, the books, the students' desks lined in their straight rows. In his wide eyes I recognized fear of not knowing what was between those book covers combined with a longing to learn what the pages held.

Each time I gave him a good report, he beamed and said, "Darryl's a good boy. Now, Willie, he's a different story. But Darryl, that boy never gives me any trouble."

When I got to Darryl's desk, he lapped up the attention
like a starving child. He had no mother, and I knew he
craved the maternal touch. "Good work, Darryl," I said,
and he looked up at me, his face shining with pride.

CHAPTER FIVE

"All brains and blood are the same color" was one of my favorite quotes to hang on the bulletin board in my classroom.

The cork wall I had requested my first year at Mebane made the perfect place to scatter motivational messages among the children's artwork. Every six weeks, I redesigned the bulletin boards, and Darryl loved to help.

We cut letters out of donated wrapping paper I collected from stores around town. So that the letters would last more than one year, I laminated them -- a trick that got a mixed reaction from my principal.

"First thing you know, you're going to be laminating the toilet paper," the principal complained one time when I stopped by the office to use the laminating equipment.

The next day, I showed up at his office with all the toilet paper I could carry.

"Sorry, sir, but we've run out of laminating material."

Darryl and the other children loved the joke and laughed about it for days.

Even though Darryl wasn't a good reader, he tried to make sure his name appeared on the "Read a Tale for my Tail" bulletin board. After each child had read a book and given an oral book report, I wrote his name on a circle and added it to the tail. At the end of the year, I took all of their circles down and gave them to the children so they knew what books they'd read – or skimmed.

Darryl struggled. He didn't want to read out loud because he knew he was so far behind the other children. I didn't let him give up and tried to assign the simplest paragraphs for him to read.

Darryl made up for his slowness in reading with a natural athletic ability and put his heart in every game he played. I took one look at the size of Darryl's hands and said to myself, "That boy was made to play basketball." Our mutual love of sports was like a bridge that spanned the oceans of gender, age and race.

The other children also recognized Darryl's strengths on the field, and he was frequently among the first to be chosen for a team.

Every day I led the children in calisthenics and then we headed outside to play kickball in the field farthest from the school building. At first the children didn't believe I was really going to get out there with them in my school dress, but I laced up my Keds and off we went -- even on days when most teachers would have probably stayed inside.

My theory was that a little drizzle or cold never hurt anybody.

When the bell rang to signal the end of phys. ed., I formed a line of boys, and they raced to the building. As soon as they got inside the door, I joined the line of girls and ran in with them.

School bells were the bane of my existence until I got used to them. Ringing to signal time to go to library. Ringing to go to art class. Ringing to go to music class or to lunch.

And worse than the bells was the noise of rowdy children lined up at the water fountain on the wall outside my classroom. The hall sounded like halftime at a football game. The noise of one student screaming that another had pushed ahead of him in line echoed off those wood floors like they each held a bullhorn.

Darryl never pushed. His grandfather had trained him to be polite, and he was. But, at the same time, he was like an animal that would fight to protect itself, and the other children knew that about him.

No matter what I asked him to do, Darryl did it. No matter what he was doing, he dropped it to help me. No matter what I tried to teach him, he did the very best he could.

I liked to roam around my classroom while the children worked. I stopped at their desks, patted them on their backs and commented on their good work.

When I got to Darryl's desk, he lapped up the attention like a starving child. He had no mother, and I knew he craved the maternal touch.

"Good work, Darryl," I said, and he looked up at me, his face shining with pride.

I knew the importance of rewarding work well done – a lesson taught to me as a child studying in a one-room schoolhouse.

Back then, I walked two miles to school with my cousin Barbara, my Aunt Jean and a neighbor. On cold mornings, we huddled beside the potbelly stove to get warm. And even on the coldest days, we had to trudge through the snow to the outhouse to do our business.

Getting an education in those days was hard work.

It was Miss Mattie who gave me my first teaching job as a nine-year-old. When I advanced beyond my third grade lessons halfway through the year, she taught me fourth grade work. The next year, when I had already learned everything my class was working on, she asked me to teach the first and second graders.

From that point on, I knew I would be a teacher.

Every Friday, Miss Mattie brought a box of store-bought apples wrapped in purple paper. Times were tough during those days, and she couldn't afford to give us each an apple, so she cut them and gave us each a half.

At Mebane, I followed Miss Mattie's example, and, every Friday during the last hour of class, I rewarded my students with games of Bingo. I made sure everybody won so they could take home a little bag of candy.

All during the week, I collected leftover lunch money and used it to buy the candy so the children felt like they were contributing to the big event.

The problem was mice. Hoards of them descended on the school at night and ate the candy I hid in the closets.

I bought some mousetraps and set them in the closet, but I wasn't very happy about having to empty the traps in the mornings.

"I'll do it for you, Ms. North," Darryl volunteered one day when I complained about having to handle the dead mice.

Early every morning, after he finished his newspaper route, he came to school so that he could check the traps, take the tiny stiff corpses outside to the dumpster and reset the traps for me.

During those times alone together, Darryl talked to me about things he had never shared, and we became friends.

Many times his stories were about Willie and the latest trouble he had gotten into. I could tell Darryl was worried about his brother – especially when he felt himself used as a scapegoat.

"Darryl, what's on your mind?" I asked one morning.

"My grandfather gave me a whupping yesterday, and it's not fair," he said.

"What happened?"

"He told me and Willie to mow the grass. I was supposed to cut half, and Willie was supposed to cut half. I did my part and left to go play, and when I came home, Willie had told my grandfather that he had cut the only half that was mowed. I got the whupping."

"I'm sorry, Darryl. Sometimes life isn't always fair," I said and tried to make it better with a hug.

* * *

Thirty days before the end of school, I started winding my class down.

To help the children count down the days until summer vacation, I hung a picture of a kangaroo with a long tail on the bulletin board with the words, "A snip a day takes the tail away." Each day we snipped a piece of tail off to mark our progress toward the last class.

For each of those 30 days, a student was chosen in alphabetical order to be "King" or "Queen for the Day." The king or queen sat in a special chair at the front of the room while I read the poem I had written especially for him or her and presented each with my snapshot. We put their pictures and poems on the "Snip a Day" bulletin board to be collected on the last day of school.

When it came time for Darryl to be king, he balked. He didn't want me to put his picture on the board, and, when he sat in the chair to hear his poem, he slumped as far down as he could possibly slump. His eyes never left the floor.

I knew that Darryl didn't feel that leaving me was something to be celebrated, and I hoped my poem would cheer him up.

"To Darryl," I read

> *Your being in my class has been a pleasure all mine.*
> *You're a fine young man who's ever so kind.*
> *You tried your very best; there was no doubt*
> *Always helpful to me as anyone about.*
> *Sixth grade has been your best year so far;*
> *I hope nothing your happiness will mar.*
> *Much success I wish for you along the way,*

Hoping to see you again on a future day.

Love,
Ms. North

When Darryl finally lifted his head during the last few lines, I saw that his eye lashes were wet, and he lingered a little longer over the hug I gave him before he went back to his seat in the middle of the classroom.

On the last day of school, I stood at the door and, as the students walked by me, I handed them their poems and copies of my picture and gave them their last hug and a kiss good-bye.

When Darryl finally arrived in front of me, I knew I'd probably never see him again. I fought back tears with a joke.

"Have a good summer, mouse hunter," I said and hugged him goodbye.

CHAPTER SIX

Tommy Andrews opened the door to the visiting room to indicate that my first jailhouse visit with Darryl had ended.

"Darryl, you're lucky to have this woman on your side," he said.

Darryl lifted his head and looked the deputy sheriff straight in the eye.

"I know I am, sir," he said through the smile I remembered so well.

"You keep your chin up," I called after him as he walked away. "This is going to be over one of these days."

Never in my most horrible nightmare did I imagine that "one of these days" would be almost 20 years later.

Life is so much easier if you don't know what lies ahead.

That trip to the jailhouse became part of my routine during the next nine months. My visits with Darryl were awkward. He'd never been much of a conversationalist, and being in jail hadn't helped. We struggled to find something to talk about.

Each time I sat with Darryl Hunt in the Forsyth County Jail, I did what I knew how to do best. I taught.

"Look at me, Darryl," I reminded him over and over. "Remember to look at the jury. Look at the lawyers. Look at them like you're an innocent man."

Darryl told me that Mrs. Mitchell had been visiting him, as well as his two court-appointed lawyers, Gordon Jenkins and Mark Rabil.

On New Year's Eve, I called the law firm of Jenkins, Lucas, Babb & Rabil and asked to speak to either Mr. Jenkins or Mr. Rabil.

Mark Rabil returned my call on January 2, and I explained that I had been Darryl Hunt's sixth grade teacher, believed in his innocence and had spent the holidays trying to locate people I thought might be able to help with the defense.

As I thought about all the people who knew Darryl, one of the first names that came to mind was Barry Sales, one of his classmates at Mebane.

Barry's fifth grade teacher had warned me about him a few days before I was scheduled to meet him in class. He had spent part of the year before on probation and had a reputation for being a real troublemaker.

I assured her that I would handle Barry, and I did. Within a few weeks, he had warmed to my affectionate teaching approach and had become one of my favorite students and one of Darryl's best friends. Barry lived next door to Darryl's grandfather, and the boys spent many afternoons lifting weights on Barry's back porch or playing in their yards.

I had kept up with Barry after he left Mebane and had heard that he was home on Christmas break from North Carolina Central University and working at The Casual Male at Marketplace Mall.[3]

I drove over one evening to talk to him about Darryl.

"There's no way he could have stabbed that woman," Barry said. "He knew who murdered his own mama and didn't kill them. Most boys in the projects would have taken a knife to that person, but not Darryl. He just doesn't have it in him."

---

[3] Barry Sales works now as a Forsyth County deputy sheriff.

I shared Barry's opinion with Mark Rabil but also the bad news that I hadn't been able to convince any of Darryl's other teachers to come forward -- even though they believed he was innocent.

"You're a courageous woman to try to help him," Mark said.

"Darryl Hunt's special to me," I said. "But he's got three strikes against him. He's black. He's poor. And now he's in trouble."

* * *

Mark told me that Larry Little, city alderman from the North Ward, was looking for witnesses to appear in the trial.

Larry had met Darryl playing basketball at the YMCA. He knew that the boy didn't work and that he spent his days drinking with Sammy Mitchell. But, like me, he recognized a peacefulness in Darryl that would have made it impossible for him to kill Deborah Sykes.

He had also seen the police composites and insisted that none of them looked like Darryl. Thomas Murphy, who saw a man with Sykes before the attack, had provided the description for one. William Hooper, who was driving to work and said he saw two men with her, provided the details used for two more. None pictured a man with skin as dark as Darryl's. None showed a man wearing cornrows.

Larry had visited Darryl's 14-year-old white girlfriend, Margaret "Little Bit" Crawford, in the detention center in Atlanta, and heard her say that police had tried to bully her into incriminating Darryl.

He believed that an innocent man was going to trial for a murder he didn't commit and organized the Darryl Hunt Defense Committee to raise money through local churches.

I had mixed feelings about Mr. Little.

I knew Darryl needed powerful people helping him, but I wasn't so sure the founder of the North Carolina Chapter of the Black Panther Party was the right kind of help.

I feared that some of the white jurors might look at Larry and remember the newspaper photograph taken of him in 1970. He was pictured with a rifle, standing guard behind Polly Graham as the Panthers protested her eviction. I felt sure that if that image crossed the minds of the jury, Darryl would suffer.

The Thursday before the trial was to begin, I visited Darryl.

Unlike our previous visits, he started talking almost before he got inside the room.

"Ms. North, they put me in a lineup yesterday," he said.

"A lineup? This close to the trial?"

"Yeah. They lined me and some other guys up in the hall and somebody in the elevator looked through the window at us."

"Do you know who it was?"

"No, ma'am. We couldn't see through the window."

"That doesn't make sense to me. Your picture's been in the paper for nine months. Everybody in town knows what you look like."

Darryl looked like that same little boy on the first day of school. The little boy who, without opening his mouth, seemed to be saying, "I know I'm not much."

He sat slumped in the chair, staring at the floor. My insides churned, and I saw red.

I knew Darryl's attorneys had been interviewing potential witnesses for nine months but wondered how they were going to have enough time to prepare a defense against this new accuser. The trial was scheduled to begin in less than a week.

I called Mark. He said they had filed a motion to stop the lineup, but that the motion had been denied. They had gone down to the jail to be present during the lineup, but hadn't been allowed to choose the men who appeared with Darryl or to be in the elevator with the witness.

* * *

As a little girl growing up in Ashe County, North Carolina in the '30s, I had never heard the term "racial barrier," but I knew it when I saw it. And I didn't like it.

About 50 people lived in our small community of Oval, and only two of the families were black. One family we never saw, although we knew their names and where they lived. The other black family, we knew well.

Mac was a very dark-skinned man in his 50s with long arms and legs that went in all directions when he moved. Watching him walk across the yard was like watching a rubberband man.

He worked for everybody in Oval, my father included. We had such a little bit of land that it didn't pay for us to own a horse, so Mac brought his over to our place, and he and Daddy plowed the garden together. When they were finished, they went over to Mac's land and plowed his.

Every fall, Mac helped kill our hogs. We took the shoulders and the hams to town and traded them for things we needed like coffee and sugar, and we gave Mac the chitlins and the fatback.

Mac was plowing with Daddy when my three-year-old sister Peggy's little chicken, Peepee, died. When the men came up to the house for lunch, Mac saw Peggy crying and said, "What we need to do is have us a funeral for this little chicky."

After lunch, he and Peggy put the chicken in a shoebox and walked out into the yard and dug a shoebox-sized hole. They stood together, heads bowed, and Mac preached a short sermon.

"This little chicky lived a good life, and now it's gone on to heaven," he said, and then Peggy laid the box in the hole, and Mac covered it with dirt and went back to plowing.

On the Sundays when he felt the need for organized religion, Mac took his place on the back row of our sanctuary rather than worshipping with his family in the little clapboard church all the local children liked to pretend was haunted.

I didn't understand why Mac plowed with us and prayed with us but didn't eat at the same table with us.

"Why does Mac sit by himself at that table over in the corner?" I asked my mother.

"Jo Anne, he's more comfortable there."

"Mac, come eat with us," I begged, but he refused each time I asked.

And when Mother served our cornbread, instead of breaking it the way we all did, Mac always cut his with a knife so that his hands didn't touch the food we were eating.

Mac had a wife named Geneva for whom Mother quite often made clothes. Once when she was fitting Geneva for a new dress, Mother slipped with a colloquial slur, "That fits just like a nigger's hunting shirt." Mother realized her mistake and looked like she wished a hole would open up in the floor and swallow her up.

She glanced sideways at Geneva to see if she had been hurt by the careless words. Either Geneva hadn't heard, or she pretended she hadn't.

I had heard and, even though I was only 10, I felt wounded for Geneva.

And some 40 years later, when I heard that Darryl Hunt had been part of a lineup less than a week before he was to go to trial for murder, I remembered Geneva.

As much as I loved Darryl and wanted to believe
that I could help him, I had heard whites called
"nigger lover" too many times not to be afraid.

CHAPTER SEVEN

I didn't leave racial prejudice behind me when I left Ashe County in 1952.

More than thirty years later, I experienced it as a summer counselor at the Governor's School.

The School was among the pioneering public educational institutions to attempt integration in the state, and blacks were among the first 200 children accepted when it opened.

The teens didn't seem to notice color differences, but some of their parents did. On more than one occasion in the early '70s, white parents asked that their children be moved out of a room they shared with a black child. The director, Jim Bray, refused to make the change, and, once while I worked there, parents withdrew their child because of his stand.

Governor's School provided my first experience in working with a black teacher. Her name was Fannie, and she and I worked together as dormitory counselors.

Fannie amazed me by the way she could change so quickly from her black dialect to perfect English. It was almost as if somebody had flipped a switch to hear her go from "chillin," as she spoke to her own children on the phone, to "young ladies" in addressing the girls in the dorm.

Fannie never appeared in public without her wig of straight brown hair. Many nights, I knocked on Fannie's door to get help with some problem with the girls, and she'd open it before she could get the wig on straight.

All the adventures we shared during our six weeks together served to cement our friendship.

One morning at about three o'clock, a sleepy girl knocked on my door and said Fannie was doubled over with pains in her chest.

I loaded my friend into my car and headed across town to Kate Bitting Hospital, where most blacks were treated at the time. As I stopped at a red light, a rusty red pickup with two young white boys pulled up beside us in the turn lane. I saw them eye Fannie on the passenger's side.

As I pulled away from the light, the truck turned into the same lane behind me and began to tailgate us. I struggled alternately with my fear of what the boys might do and my fear of whether Fannie would die of a heart attack before I could get her to the hospital.

When I entered the hospital parking lot, the truck disappeared into the night, the cruel game over.

Fannie was diagnosed with indigestion instead of the heart attack I had imagined, but that wasn't my last hospital experience with her. And it wasn't the worst.

Later that school year, Fannie pulled her car out of her driveway and into the path of a truck. An ambulance rushed her to Kate Bitting again but immediately transferred her to one of the larger hospitals with better doctors and equipment.

She was admitted on Wednesday, and I went to see her on Friday.

When I walked into her room, what I saw almost knocked me off my feet. After two days lying in that hospital bed, Fannie's hair was still matted with dried blood.

I ran out into the hall and called for a nurse.

"What's the problem?" a young woman asked.

"This woman in here needs cleaning up. Do I need to do it, or are you?"

"We'll get to her."

"Maybe I need to see the head nurse. I can't understand why it's not already been done. This is a human being here."

"I said we'll get to it," she said

"No, I want it done now," I said, raising my voice a few decibels. The increased volume apparently got her attention. Within a few minutes, a team of nurses arrived.

I stood outside the door while Fannie was being bathed, and after her room emptied of hospital staff, walked back inside and sat on the side of the bed.

Stroking the closely cropped black hair my friend had always kept hidden under the wig, I asked her if she needed anything else before I left.

"Come back," she said and smiled.[4]

* * *

During that same time, I saw very little racial prejudice among the orphans I taught at the Children's Home in Winston-Salem. For so long, they had actually seemed unaware of the difference between the two black faculty members and the remaining dozen or so of us who were white.

When the teachers displayed our baby pictures and our current pictures on the bulletin board and held a contest to see if the children could match them, I was amused to see one little boy try to match a white baby with a black teacher.

"No, silly," his friend said. "That can't be him. His ears are too big."

---

[4] Fannie was treated for minor brain injuries, returned to teaching and died years later from causes unrelated to the accident. She and I remained close friends throughout her life.

Because that innocence seemed to pervade the Home, I was surprised some time later to see the way little Annie was treated there.

Annie was a very dark-skinned 13-year-old in the eighth grade when she came to live at the Home. I had never seen a black child sent to the orphanage. It seemed to me that extended black families preferred to care for their orphans rather than ask for help – especially from a predominantly white institution.

Annie arrived wearing a nylon stocking cap that she refused to take off. She wore it pulled down tightly over her hair everywhere she went, all the time.

One day during her first week with us, I came out the front door and noticed her standing at the bottom of the steps crying. She was surrounded by a circle of white children, all laughing at her nappy hair sticking straight up.

Keith, a tall blond seventh grader, had snatched her cap and disappeared with it.

I walked down the steps and put my arms around Annie and said, "Annie, what's wrong?"

"They took my cap."

"Who took your cap?"

"Don't know who."

"Honey, you sit down right there on that bench, and I'll be right back."

The children couldn't go far since they lived right there on campus, so it didn't take long for me to find Keith and the cap.

When I told him to take it back to Annie, he pretended to be afraid to pick it up.

Hands on hips, I said to Keith, "Were you afraid to jerk it off her head?"

Keith shifted from one foot to the other. "No, ma'am."

"Then you're not afraid to pick it up and hand it back to her."

43

Keith picked up the cap and held it out like it was a poisonous snake.

"Now, you present that hat to Annie as if it were a crown, and you apologize for embarrassing her. She's trying to fit in at this school. Can you imagine how hard that is for her?"

By that time, stealing the cap wasn't nearly as funny. As I watched him hand it to a smiling Annie, I didn't realize that I was witnessing the beginning of a friendship.

* * *

I thought about Annie and her tormentors when Mark Rabil called and said he wanted to subpoena me to appear as a character witness at Darryl's trial.

"I know that what I'm asking you to do is a frightening thing," he said, "but it would help Darryl's case a lot to have a teacher -- a white woman – take the witness stand in his defense."

I thought about Fannie still covered with blood after two days in the hospital and hesitated.

"Give me a few days to think about it," I said.

I wanted to consider what testifying for Darryl might do to me and to my family. I knew that in the south, crosses were still burned by men in white sheets.

My family was afraid for my physical safety, but I was confident that I had their support in whatever decision I made – especially my younger sister, Rita.

All of my black friends were opposed.

"Jo Anne, I don't think this is worth the price you'll have to pay," one said. "Darryl is a nobody."

"He's a *somebody* to me."

I called another one of Darryl's teachers – a black man – and asked him to go to court with me. He refused.

Even Tommy Andrews was doubtful.

"I'm not sure you can do Darryl any good," he said, "and it may hurt you."

As much as I loved Darryl and wanted to believe that I could help him, I had heard whites called "nigger lover" too many times not to be afraid.

Finally, I visited Jack Noffsinger, my minister at Knollwood Baptist Church. I knew Dr. Jack had been very active in efforts to integrate Winston-Salem, especially the churches.

"Jo Anne, I want you to realize what you're doing and what the consequences could be," he said. "Are you convinced in your heart that Darryl is innocent?"

"Yes, sir, I am."

"If you are sure that this kid is not guilty, I think that, in the future, you will regret not helping him. I think you ought to do it."

"That's all I need," I said.

* * *

I phoned Mark Rabil and told him I would be willing to take the stand in Darryl's defense.

Mark, Gordon Jenkins, Darryl and I met in the same conference room where I had visited Darryl after his arrest. I knew I was doing the right thing by testifying, and I sensed that Darryl found a lot of hope in the fact that I was going to be in the courtroom with him.

As I looked at the men whose job it was to save Darryl's life, I wondered how it felt to be carrying such a weight.

Mark had been out of law school only four years and worked in the firm where his cousin Bill Rabil was practicing real estate law. Mark and Gordon Jenkins were the only two criminal trial lawyers in the firm, but neither had ever tried a capital murder case.

Their names appeared on the Superior Court's list of lawyers willing to be appointed to represent defendants. Despite the number of attorneys eager to take Darryl's highly publicized case, Judge Alexander had appointed Gordon Jenkins. He had asked the judge to let Mark serve with him, and his request was granted.

At first, Mark and Gordon had assumed their client was guilty and that their job was to get him a life sentence instead of the death penalty. Darryl's consistency in remembering details convinced them of his innocence as much as the fact that all the evidence linking him to the crime was circumstantial.

But we all knew that anything could happen in a jury trial. Mark had polled more than 300 Forsyth County residents called for jury duty and found that whites presumed Darryl was guilty, while blacks presumed he was innocent.

Mark saw his job as saving Darryl's life. A verdict of "not guilty" was his dream.

A block from the building, I spotted the picketers. About
50 blacks waved homemade "Free Darryl Hunt" signs
in a show of support that helped to give me the courage
I needed. As I approached, the chanting grew louder.
I realized they didn't know I was on their side.

CHAPTER EIGHT

I learned early that life isn't always fair.

When I was five years old – the year before I started first grade – I made a trip to school with my Aunt Jean, who was only a few years older than I was. A little boy named Willard was absent that day, and I felt that I had been given the moon when I was allowed to sit at his desk.

"You can have those," my Aunt Jean whispered when she saw me look longingly at the boy's crayons. "Willard won't mind."

I dropped the box of crayons into my pocket and carried them home.

"Where did you get those crayons, Jo Anne?" Daddy asked when he saw me coloring after supper.

"Jean gave them to me."

Daddy grabbed me by the scruff of my neck and marched me to Jean's house.

"Those crayons belong to Willard," were her words of damnation.

"But you told me I could have them," I shrieked as Daddy began to spank me for stealing.

My father and I took the crayons back to Willard the next day, but I never forgot the stab to my heart as I heard myself being falsely accused.

Almost 50 years later, as I prepared for my first day in court during the trial of Darryl Hunt in the late spring of 1985, I remembered wailing with rage at each undeserved whack of my father's hand. The memories of powerlessness washed over me in waves.

As soon as I had received my subpoena to appear, I had begun making plans to be out of school. Since I didn't know how long I'd be absent, I prepared lesson plans for a week and made sure the substitute had a list of students scheduled to assist each day.

The night before the trial began, I tossed and turned in the bedroom across the hall from my mother.

Mother had moved to Winston-Salem in 1964, a year after she and Daddy divorced. When Charles North and I divorced in 1976, I moved in with her.[5]

During the night, my mother heard me get out of bed and followed me into the kitchen.

We sat on opposite sides of the kitchen bar, staring at each other in silence, listening to the tree frogs croaking and the clock ticking.

"Tomorrow is going to be a difficult day for you, Jo Anne," Mother finally said. "We'll probably hear some repercussions from this, and you could lose lots of your friends."

I nodded. I knew Mother supported my decision to testify but that she was as afraid as I was.

"Do one thing for me," she said. "Be as discreet as possible. The fewer people who know you're doing this, the better."

Nobody knew that better than I. I had told my close friends and family about my visits with Darryl and my role in the trial,

---

[5] Fred Vannoy died of natural causes in 1977, at the age of 62. Maude Vannoy is still living at 91.

but, at school, only the principal knew where I was going to be that week.

Finally, I said goodnight for the second time and climbed back into bed. When the alarm rang at 6 o'clock, I had just fallen back to sleep.

Mother served my toast, orange juice and coffee and sat with me at the kitchen bar as I tried to get them down my throat. We didn't talk.

I left the house at eight o'clock so I would have plenty of time to find a place to park and a seat before court began at nine.

Mother stood at the door and watched as I walked alone to my car. While she had supported my decision to witness, she never offered to go with me to court.

As I headed downtown, I didn't know what to expect.

All the way to the courthouse, I fought with my worst nightmares. Hate mail. Angry phone calls. Ugly graffiti. Burned out houses. They all followed me the short distance downtown.

I kept assuring myself that my appearance as a character witness would help Darryl Hunt. Mark Rabil had told me so over and over.

As I walked to the courthouse on May 28, 1985 to appear in the case, *State of North Carolina vs. Darryl Eugene Hunt*, I felt like a soldier going into battle.

A block from the building, I spotted the picketers. About 50 blacks waved homemade "Free Darryl Hunt" signs in a show of support that helped to give me the courage I needed. As I approached, the chanting grew louder. I realized they didn't know I was on their side.

I smiled in their direction but didn't stop to explain that I was fighting on the same side they were. I didn't want to be late.

I walked through the front door and was directed to the fifth floor courtroom. Mark was standing in the hall with his partner Gordon Jenkins and several people I hadn't met.

"Jo Anne, come here. I've got some people here I want to introduce you to," he said. He introduced the private investigator, "Slick" Poteat, and then the tall black man standing behind him.

"Larry Little, I want you to meet Jo Anne North."

Larry smiled. And as he took my hand and looked into my eyes, the image of the angry young man with the gun disappeared, and I began to soften.

"I appreciate your being here," he said. "I realize it's not an easy thing for you."

"No, sir, it's not, but I believe in Darryl's innocence."

"Yes, ma'am, we all do."

When we walked into the courtroom, it seemed to me that it was filled with blacks and that I was the only white woman there. Larry walked to the front and sat with Mr. Poteat in the row behind the defense table. Near him, I spotted Rev. Carlton Eversley, Rev. John Mendez and many of the church members who had been praying for Darryl.

I found a seat on the second row, behind the press and the prosecution so Darryl would be able to see me from his position at the defense table.

I crossed my arms tightly over my chest, trying to hold myself together.

Darryl walked in between his attorneys, Gordon Jenkins and Mark Rabil. He wore a white shirt and tie, a dark three-piece suit and looked straight ahead in the way I had coached him.

The cornrows were gone, and he wore his hair in a conservative Afro.

Scanning the courtroom, he saw me and smiled. I gave him the thumbs up sign.

* * *

During the jury selection, I watched one black after another step up to the witness stand.

"Do you believe in the death penalty?" prosecutor Don Tisdale asked, over and over.

"No."

"Cause," Mr. Tisdale responded to each.

"You may step down," Judge Preston Cornelius said so many times I lost count.

As one after another black was disqualified from serving on the jury, I felt my spirits sink. In the end, only one of the 12 jurors was black.

On my way out the door to go home for lunch, I ran into Katherine Smith, a news reporter with Channel 8 TV. I recognized her as a former president of the alumni association at Governor's School.

When Katherine asked to interview me for the 6 o'clock news, I stalled her until after lunch.

All the way home, I wrestled with whether I should talk to the media or not. When I reached home, I asked Mother what she thought.

"Not with the two of us living here alone," she said without missing a beat.

As I drove back downtown, I dreaded disappointing Katherine. When I pulled into the parking lot, my mind was still in the middle of the debate.

I swung my car too wide, and, as I pulled into an open parking space, I scraped the side of a 1957 Chevrolet that looked like the paint was still wet.

I got out and surveyed the damage. When I didn't see the owner anywhere nearby, I wrote my name and phone number on a piece of paper with a note to call me so I could pay for the damages. I stuck it on the windshield and ran into the courthouse.

Katherine stood in the hall, waiting for me.

"I'm really sorry, but I just can't do it," I said. "The way so many people feel about the trial, I'm afraid somebody would burn my house down if they saw me on television."

Relieved that she didn't push me, I sat down on a bench in the hallway and began to work on the vest I was crocheting. The repetitive motion of the needlework seemed to calm me, and the yarn lay in my lap like a security blanket.

Within a few minutes, a red-faced sheriff's deputy stomped over.

"Excuse me, ma'am, but you need to return to the jury room," he said.

"But I'm not on the jury."

"Then why are you here?" he demanded.

"I'm here as a character witness for the defense."

The man looked me up and down, turned on his heel and left without another word.

When I returned from lunch the next day, I felt like I had walked into the chill of a meat locker. The courthouse staff -- people who had laughed and joked with me days before -- now took my pocketbook and my knitting bag and dumped everything out. They opened my makeup kit and jerked out a pair of small nail scissors.

"What are these for?" one of the men snarled.

"They're fingernail scissors," I said, dumbfounded at the way I was being treated. I had served on three juries before and had never been searched.

When I looked up and saw the sheriff's deputy who had mistaken me for a member of the jury the day before, I understood.

I felt myself drawn even closer to the man I was there to defend.

The use of Sammy Mitchell's name during the 911
call had started that train heading in his friend
Darryl Hunt's direction, and it didn't seem like
anybody was having much luck stopping it.

CHAPTER NINE

On Tuesday, June 3, the State began to present its case against Darryl Eugene Hunt, calling Deborah Sykes' mother, Evelyn Jefferson, to the witness stand.

Mrs. Jefferson's hair was elegantly coifed, and her makeup looked like an advertisement for Lancome, but it was the horror in her eyes that everybody in the courtroom saw. She didn't speak long, but every word she uttered in her raspy southern drawl turned sharp with anger and seemed like a nail in Darryl's coffin. I watched several members of the jury dab their eyes as she tried to compose herself enough to answer a few questions about the older of her two daughters.

I had never had children of my own, but I tried to imagine what she had felt when she heard that her daughter had been murdered. How she felt that day when she thought about the fact that she would never see Deborah again. What she felt when she looked at the man sitting 10 feet away from her at the defense table. The man accused of stabbing and raping her child.

I looked at Darryl and was proud to see his straight back and his head held high throughout her testimony and the parade of witnesses who followed her to the stand.

I listened to Fred Flagler, the *Journal* editor. Almost a year later, his frustration was still palpable as he described calling the police shortly after 11 a.m. on the day of the murder to report a missing person. About being transferred from a dispatcher to a supervisor who told him to get in touch with her family. Instead, he called Police Chief Lucius Powell and was met at the scene of the crime by Detective Daulton.

Ethel Wiggins, the police department communications operator, testified about taking a call at 6:53 a.m. from a man who identified himself as "Sammy Mitchell" and said he saw an attack near the fire station downtown. Instead of the station near Crystal Towers where the attack occurred, she said officers were sent to Claremont Avenue.

I listened to Brian Watts' story of walking downtown between shifts at the Adele Knits plant on Chatham Road and finding a pocketbook, sandals and sweater lying on the ground near the wood fence. I gritted my teeth as he described discovering the bloody body, naked from the waist down. I looked over at Darryl. He appeared calmer than I felt.

Even when Detective Daulton, the lead investigator, took the stand, Darryl didn't duck his head.

Daulton described receiving a call from Chief Powell's office around noon August 10 and said that he called Flagler and met him about 20 minutes later at Deborah's abandoned car. He said he went back to his office, made calls to the hospitals and then returned to the scene. He knocked on doors in the area and met Watts, who said he had found a body. Daulton pointed to the places on a map where the body, purse, sandals and slacks were found.

He admitted that no knife or any other evidence had ever been found that would link Darryl to the murder of Deborah Sykes.

Darryl stared straight ahead as Lew Stringer, the local medical examiner, described the stab wounds; as Michael Shkrum, the

Chapel Hill medical examiner, confirmed rape and sodomy; and as Brenda Dew, of the North Carolina State Bureau of Investigation, called the tests of the hair and semen samples "inconclusive."

The last person to take the stand that day was Bobby Upchurch, a painter who had told police he saw a black man attack a white woman but couldn't identify the victim or the attacker or provide a description of either.

At the end of the first day, I felt encouraged by the lack of physical evidence. As Darryl was escorted from the courtroom, he looked my way, and I gave him another thumbs-up sign.

We smiled.

* * *

Within the first few minutes of the next day's testimony, I lost some of my confidence.

Thomas Murphy, wearing a light blue short-sleeved shirt, took the stand. He said that on his way to work at the Hanes Dye and Finishing plant on August 10, he had observed a woman talking with a black man and thought he was seeing another white woman gone wrong. He had called the police as soon as he heard about the murder on the evening news.

That night he had looked through mug shots, didn't see a familiar face but was able to put together a police composite of a black man with medium brown skin. I looked at Darryl and trusted the jury saw the same dark black complexion I did.

Eighteen days after the murder, Murphy signed a statement that he saw Sykes with a black man. Four weeks after the murder, he identified Darryl from about half a dozen photographs.

Despite the fact that Mr. Murphy admitted being a former alcoholic and member of the Ku Klux Klan, I was afraid that his story presented doubt in Darryl's innocence. He seemed so confident that Darryl was the man he had seen attacking Deborah Sykes as he pointed his finger at him in the courtroom.

The next witness was Johnny Gray, a surly looking drink house[6] regular who remained on the stand for the rest of the day.

He said he had been walking on West End Boulevard and heard a woman screaming behind the wood fence. He peered over and saw a black man straddling a white woman. When questioned about why he used the name "Sammy Mitchell" when he called 911, he said he didn't want to get involved and used the first name that popped into his head.

On August 22, he had identified Terry Thomas as the man he saw at the crime scene, but his identification didn't hold when police discovered that Thomas had been in jail at the time of the murder.

As Judge Cornelius dismissed court for the day, I realized I was growing weary already and wondered how long the trial would last. Sitting still was torture for somebody like me who spent my days moving around the classroom. Added to my natural restlessness was the sensation of watching a speeding train barreling down on a helpless man.

The use of Sammy Mitchell's name during the 911 call had started that train heading in his friend Darryl Hunt's direction, and it didn't seem like anybody was having much luck stopping it.

* * *

By the third day of the prosecution's presentation, the picketers knew who I was. I spotted a former student named Sheila in the crowd and knew that she must have assured them that I was not part of the press or a member of Deborah Sykes' family. I was Ms. North, the white woman who had taught Darryl Hunt.

Suddenly, I was their ally, and they cheered me as a hero going into another day's battle. And with each passing day, I needed those cheers more and more.

---

[6] In southern black communities, a drink house is a residential home open for the illegal sale of alcohol by the drink.

On June 5, I heard testimony from Roger Weaver, the smooth-talking, fancy-dressing hotel auditor Darryl had told me identified him in a lineup the week before the trial.

On the morning of the murder, Weaver, a white man, was working at the Hyatt House Hotel. He saw a black man go into the restroom and sent a security guard in to ask him to leave. When Weaver went in some time later, he found pink water drops in the sink and bloody paper towels in the trash.

When he saw Darryl's picture in the paper a month after the crime, he was sure he was the man he saw go into the restroom. Afraid for his own safety, Weaver waited until September 19 to go to the police.

The next witness, hotel security guard Danny Holt, actually saw the man leave the restroom, but couldn't make an identification.

That raised my hopes – at least for a short while. The next few witnesses confused me, and I wondered what they might be doing to the jury.

Dennis Speaks, another drink house regular, testified that he heard Darryl and Sammy talking about Deborah Sykes, but said he thought the police were trying to frame them.

Darryl's white girlfriend Margaret Crawford was on the witness stand most of the day. As I looked at her, I realized she was the same age as some of my middle school children, but her eyes looked like they had seen much more than the average 14-year-old.

I knew she had seen the inside of a courtroom more than once, but the way she bit her fingernails and spun around in her chair led me to believe that at least some small part of her felt fear at finding herself in a murder trial.

The girl said that during her own arrest September 11 on charges of larceny and failure to appear, she signed two statements under pressure.

In the first statement, she had said that Darryl and Sammy Mitchell had spent the night of August 9 with her at the Motel

6, about five miles from the murder scene, and that they had left about six o'clock the next morning in a cab. She said Darryl came back at about 9:30 with grass stains on his pants and that he seemed nervous and said he needed a drink.

In her second statement, she had said Darryl had told her Sammy raped and killed Sykes.

I was relieved to hear her deny the statements, but my heart sank as I listened to Detective Debbie Gatto's testimony that Larry Little had told the girl not to talk.

I looked around for Larry but didn't see him. Several times during the trial, I observed him rush from the courtroom and reappear some time later looking more composed. I assumed he was in the lobby again, walking off steam.

I could almost feel everyone in the courtroom cringe as the prosecution called its last witness – the victim's husband, Douglas Sykes.

I had not been able to identify with Deborah's mother, but I could identify with her husband. I was sure everyone in the courtroom could. My emotions surged from embarrassment to grief to anger as he testified about the last time he had made love to his wife.

"I don't want $12,000 if I have to lie," Darryl had said even -- when Tisdale had told him he would push for the death penalty. I couldn't help but agree with Mark's comment, "You know, Jo Anne, most people would have taken that offer."

CHAPTER TEN

After the lunch break on June 6, the defense called its first witness, Robert Archer.

Mr. Archer was a retired officer who had worked with the Winston-Salem Police Department for 28 years. He testified that he was still working on August 22, 1984, when Johnny Gray had pointed out a man he said was involved in the Sykes murder. The man had gotten on a bus before Mr. Archer could reach him, nor could he identify him.

Expert witness Robert Buckout drilled into the jury the pitfalls of eye-witness identification. He described the dangers inherent in letting too much time lapse between the incident and the identification and in white people incorrectly identifying a black person.

Ronald Wiles, Johnny Gray's neighbor, and Rayford Thompson, his landlord, both testified that Gray told them the police had promised him money for testifying.

Lisa McBride, Johnny Gray's girlfriend, testified that he told her about the murder the day after it occurred and talked about picking out two men in the line-up. She said that Gray told her he was going to get half the reward money for testifying. Mark asked her if Gray had ever hurt her, and she said he had stabbed her in the shoulder after threatening to stab her in the heart. Her mother, Mary McBride, verified her daughter's relationship with Gray.

Gene Foster, Gray's friend, said Gray identified a different man as the murderer. Therapists Darcena Nahigyan and David Steele both said Margaret Crawford was not truthful. Capt. John O'Brian, the jail administrator, said he had no problems with Darryl in jail and that Darryl's isolation had been for his own protection.

Allen Lambert, the assistant clerk of Superior Court, described the court docket for August 10, 1984, showing that Sammy Mitchell's case had been continued to August 24. There was no indication as to whether he was in court or that Darryl had a case in court on August 10.

Next, Detective Daulton took the stand. He described the money paid to Johnny Gray for testifying; $10 on August 10; $20 on August 24; $70 on August 29; $10 on August 29; and $100 on January 22, 1985. All the money came from the police department information fund. No money was to be paid by Crimestoppers until the case was closed. He said nobody ever promised Johnny Gray any Crimestoppers money and that Gray insisted he wasn't testifying in exchange for the reward money.

Daulton described going to the crime scene with Gray and pointed out on a map where he and Murphy were when they saw the suspected man or men. He said he had also talked to all the residents of Crystal Towers and others in the area -- at least 400 people, including about 30 –40 black men. Five to ten of those men wore their hair in cornrows, he said, admitting that Darryl was the only one in the photo lineup with cornrows.

I smiled when Mattie Mitchell took the stand. Here was someone who I knew must love Darryl almost as much as I did. I had heard that she visited him in jail more than she did her own son, Sammy.

Mrs. Mitchell testified that she had seen Darryl and Sammy the morning of the murder, wearing the same clothes they had on the day before. She saw no grass stains, mud or blood on anything they were wearing.

* * *

During a break, a young black sheriff's deputy beckoned for me to join him at the side of the room.

"You're going to testify this afternoon, aren't you?" he said.

"Yes, and I'm very nervous."

"I'll tell you what to do," he whispered. "I'm going to walk halfway back in the courtroom, and when you take the stand, you look at me whenever you get nervous. Don't look at Darryl, or you'll get upset."

I thanked him and sat down beside the same woman I'd been sitting next to every day. I didn't know who she was, and she didn't know why I was there. We had made small talk but had never discussed our roles in the case.

As I sat down, she turned and looked at me.

"Why are you here?" she demanded.

"I'm a character witness for the defense," I said. "I taught Darryl."

Without a word, the woman I later learned was Deborah Sykes' aunt moved further down the row to sit next to the rest of the family.

* * *

When Mark Rabil called me, I was barely able to walk to the witness stand without falling flat on my face.

The young black sheriff's deputy, who had spoken to me earlier, stood at the side of the courtroom with his hands clasped behind him. He stared straight at me and smiled.

I focused on his face and felt my breathing slow.

After I had been sworn in, Don Tisdale asked to approach the bench.

I heard him tell Judge Cornelius that he didn't think I was a credible witness. I hadn't been associated with the defendant in seven years, and Darryl had changed during that time, he argued. He said he was afraid I was going to testify that Darryl was innocent.

I wasn't surprised. Mark Rabil had warned me that the prosecution would try to keep me from the stand.

"I don't think she'd be here if she thought he were guilty," Judge Cornelius said and denied the request to keep me from testifying.

"Then I refuse to cross-examine her," Don said. "I'll let Mr. Lyle do it."

As Mark stood up to begin his questioning, I glanced at my beacon at the back of the room before I directed my attention to Mark.

"State your name."

"Jo Anne North."

"What do you do?"

"I am a public school teacher."

"What grade?"

"Sixth grade at Philo Middle School."

"How long?"

"That's a terrible question to ask a lady," I joked and then told him I'd taught 29 years.

"Have you been there that long in Forsyth County?"

"No, sir. I taught one year in Miami."

"Do you know Darryl Hunt?"

"I know Darryl Hunt and have for years."

"When did you first meet?"

"I taught Darryl Hunt in 1975-76."

"Have you seen him since?"

"Yes, I have."

"Do you remember when you saw him?"

"I went to visit him when he was incarcerated."

"How many times?"

"Three."

"Have you spoken to anybody about this case regarding Darryl?"

"Yes."

"Who?"

"Anyone that would listen."

"Have you spoken to anybody involved in the case?"

"The first person I called when I saw Darryl Hunt's picture in the paper was the District Attorney."

"What was the purpose of that call?"

"Objection," Mr. Lyle shouted. I almost leaped out of my seat.

Judge Cornelius overruled his objection.

"Ms. North, do you have an opinion as to Darryl's character for being a truthful person?"

"Objection," Mr. Lyle shouted again.

"Overruled."

"I can only give you a basis of Darryl Hunt when he was 13 years old," I said. "My opinion when he was in my class, that being six hours a day, 180 days a year, and that he was a mild mannered sixth grader."

Mr. Lyle objected again. "Not responsive."

"Sustained," Judge Cornelius ordered gently.

"Have you seen him since then?"

"Yes."

"Has your opinion changed at all since then?"

"Objection. Not given an opinion."

"Sustained."

"Do you have a present opinion as to Darryl's character for truthfulness."

"Yes, I do."

"What is that opinion?"

"My opinion is that Darryl Hunt is not that sort of person."

"Objection."

"Sustained. Members of the jury, disregard the response of the witness."

"I'm trying to ask you if you think he's a truthful person."

"I certainly think he is. I had no reason to think he would lie to me, and I have students that I have to decide that all the time."

"Do you have a present opinion as to Darryl Hunt's character for being a peaceful person?"

"Objection."

"Until you lay the foundation on what it's based on," Judge Cornelius said. "Three times visiting the jail, is that it?"

"And her prior knowledge," Mark said.

"From 1976. Objection," Mr. Lyle said.

"Thank you, Ms. North," Mark said.

"No questions," Mr. Lyle said.

"That's all for Ms. North," Mark said.

Judge Cornelius recessed the jury for lunch.

As I stepped down from the witness stand to return to my seat, I looked at Darryl and saw tears on his cheeks. As I felt my own eyes begin to fill, I knew why the sheriff's deputy had told me not to look at Darryl during my testimony.

I walked out of the courtroom, out of the courthouse and over to the parking lot. A piece of paper was tucked under the windshield of my car.

Opening it, I read "Go home, nigger lover" in red ink smeared like blood across the tattered piece of lined notebook paper.

My hands shook as I drove home with the day's proceedings still running through my mind.

"How did it go," Mother asked when I walked through the front door.

"I think it went very well," I said. I didn't tell her about the note or about the hang-up call the night before. I didn't want her to sit at home alone with the same fear I felt in my heart. "I really don't see how they can find him guilty," I said with all the confidence I could muster.

A voice in my head reminded me of the almost all-white jury.

* * *

The next day, I went back to school. I had agreed with my principal that I would return to class as soon as possible. I felt I had made an important contribution to Darryl's case and that my work in the courtroom had been accomplished. I needed to get back to the work in my classroom.

There was only one testimony I hated to miss and that was Darryl's. I called Mark the evening after he took the stand.

Mark said I would have been proud. Darryl had answered questions about where he was at the time of the murder; about meeting with the police to listen to the 911 tape from "Sammy Mitchell" and several other times to answer their questions. He had said Tisdale had offered him $12,000 and told him he could go free if he would say that Sammy had killed Sykes.

"I don't want $12,000 if I have to lie," Darryl had said even when Tisdale had told him he would push for the death penalty.

I couldn't help but agree with Mark's comment, "You know, Jo Anne, most people would have taken that offer."

* * *

The next time I talked to Mark was on the evening of June 14, 1985. He called to tell me that, after 15 ½ hours of deliberation during three days, the jury had found Darryl guilty of first-degree murder.

I wasn't prepared to hear the word "guilty." I had shielded myself against the possibility of that verdict for so long that, when I heard it, I still didn't feel the impact.

But when I finally let my guard down several hours later, a giant boulder landed on my chest. Where my heart was.

Mark said the sentencing hearing had begun at two o'clock that afternoon and that he wanted to subpoena me to appear on Monday for the rest of the hearing. He said he didn't need me to take the stand again.

"You've done your job," he said, "but I want the jury to see you sitting there. I want them to remember that a respected person in the community believes Darryl is innocent."

The next morning I read the *Journal's* coverage of the last day of the trial.

When the verdict had been read by the Clerk of Court, Darryl "wiped tears from his eyes;" his supporters "sobbed quietly" or "sat stunned or covered their faces with their hands." The victim's family "sobbed silently." One woman on the jury "wept openly."

When each of the jurors stood to confirm their own decision, the lone black juror was the only one who had looked at Hunt.

"What I want now is the other one," Evelyn Jefferson had said, still believing that Darryl didn't act alone.

I read that the jury had been deadlocked 10-2 and had asked Judge Cornelius to explain again the legal definitions of "reasonable doubt" and "burden of proof."

He told them that the State was required to prove that Darryl was guilty but that the defense didn't have to prove that he was innocent. Reasonable doubt, he said, does not mean "beyond a shadow of a doubt." It means "doubt based on reason or common sense."

The article recapped the trial, describing Johnny Gray, who had called 911 to report the crime; Roger Weaver, the hotel auditor who identified Darryl as the man who left the blood-stained towels.

The reporter wrote that there was no physical evidence to link Darryl to the crime and that a medical expert testified that tests to match blood types from fluid samples taken from Ms. Sykes' body were "inconclusive."

That the defense had established an alibi for Darryl and discredited witness statements. That Darryl had taken the stand and denied any part in the crime and said that investigators had offered to set him free and pay him $12,000 in reward money if he would implicate Sammy Mitchell.

That Sammy had testified, confirming that he and Darryl had been at a house on South Dunleith Avenue at the time of the murder.

That a psychiatrist had called Darryl "a peaceful man, incapable of the violence."

About 75 of Darryl's supporters had sat through all 14 days of the trial and agreed that the state didn't present enough evidence for conviction.

That at least 13 armed guards and up to 100 plainclothes police were in the courtroom and on rooftops in downtown. Watching.

As soon as Judge Cornelius recessed court, Darryl's supporters had "burst through the double doors into the lobby."

Sammy Mitchell, who had been waiting there, had to be restrained by at least seven friends when he saw his mother come through the doors sobbing.

Larry Little was quoted as yelling above the crowds, "Let's keep our heads. Let's just keep our heads. Let's go to church and pray."

The crowd of supporters had run to Lloyd's Presbyterian Church at Seventh and Chestnut Streets, where they had met frequently and had gone to pray before the sentencing hearing.

Several women collapsed and had to be carried outside. One had to be restrained. Another sobbed, "I can't believe that black man (the juror) didn't see the lies."

As I read that sentence, I knew that I would have joined those women if I had been in the courtroom when the verdict was read. They would have had to carry me out, too, and I would have had to live with the embarrassment of collapsing after I had spent so long standing strong. I was grateful that my weeping had been private.

The reporter wrote that the victim's relatives waited in a private room for the crowds to leave and quoted Mrs. Jefferson as saying, "It was hard to sit there looking at him." She praised Don Tisdale for doing a good job "considering what you had to work with."

Douglas Sykes said that he was surprised that jurors deliberated for as long as they did.

When court reconvened at 2 p.m., defense attorneys began calling witnesses to the stand -- witnesses they hoped would convince jurors to sentence Hunt to life in prison. Jurors who had already said they believed in the death penalty.

Among some of the witnesses who testified were Allen H. Johnson III, the executive editor of the *Winston-Salem Chronicle*, and Alderman Larry Womble, both of whom visited Hunt in jail and said he was "calm while he maintained his innocence." Darryl's half-sister Juanita Johnson said he often helped her pay her bills and helped take care of her children.

Gordon Jenkins was quoted as saying, "I won't argue about his innocence, but I will argue that he is a person worth saving."

Pushing for the death penalty, Tisdale said, "He is no longer the defendant or the suspect. He is the murderer."

I suffered another sleepless night.

"Some day this will be over," I told Darryl. "If not in this life, in the next. Some day the world will know that you are not guilty."

CHAPTER ELEVEN

On Monday afternoon, I sat in the middle of a courtroom filled once again mostly with blacks. The guilty verdict had erased the dividing line I had felt at the beginning of the trial. Now, I felt one with them as we faced the tragedy together.

Once more, I positioned myself behind the prosecutor's table so the jury would have to look at the person who believed in Darryl's innocence and so that he could find me easily if he turned around and looked.

Again, when Darryl was brought in, he scanned the courtroom until he saw me. I smiled but kept my hands clasped in my lap this time. It's hard to give thumbs-up to a man who's been found guilty of first-degree murder.

Don Tisdale argued for the death penalty. Mark fought for Darryl's life.

The next day, I read in the *Journal* that Darryl had been sentenced to life in prison.

The jury had deliberated four hours over a list of 25 issues that it was to consider in showing mercy on Hunt. There wasn't a single vote for death. The jury had too many doubts about his guilt.

Since I had been so blindsided by the guilty verdict, I had prepared myself to hear that he had been given a death sentence.

As I read the article, I could actually feel every muscle in my body let go. Relax like I had been the one facing the electric volts.

I drove downtown to see Darryl in the jail that afternoon, hoping to visit with him before he was transferred to the prison in Raleigh.

This visit was different than the ones before the trial. Instead of going to see a man *accused* of murder, I was going to see a man *convicted* of murder. Twelve people had all agreed that Darryl Hunt had raped, sodomized and murdered Deborah Sykes.

During this visit, I did not sit alone in a room with Darryl. I was not able to touch him. To hug him.

Instead, I sat on a stool on one side of a cold, hard glass partition, and he sat on the other. Our only connection was a telephone line.

I still believed that Darryl Hunt was innocent and that the wrong man was going to prison for life.

I recognized the inmate on the stool next to Darryl as a Mebane student named "King." He hadn't been in my class, but he was the kind of likeable child everybody knows. In 1985, he was accused of murdering two people.

King kept buzzing around Darryl like a gnat.

He grabbed the phone away from Darryl. "Ms. North, you need to talk to me," he bellowed into the telephone mouthpiece. Darryl rolled his eyes and pushed him away.

Darryl and I laughed, relieved to have the distraction.

I looked into his eyes. They were dry. I kept dabbing mine with a knotty Kleenex.

"Darryl, you know you are guilty," I finally said.

"But, Ms. North - - -."

"You are guilty of choosing your friends."

Darryl knew I meant Sammy Mitchell. He seemed to think for a minute and then said, "You choose who chooses you, Ms. North. I had nobody, and Mrs. Mitchell took me in and treated me like I was her son. She was good to me."

"Well, there isn't anything either you or I can do now," I said. "How do you feel about the trial?"

Darryl Hunt didn't rant and rave about the injustice of the system. Didn't blame his lawyers. Didn't blame racism. "There's got to be a reason why 12 people thought I was guilty," he said.

"I don't know what the reason was, but right now I'm asking you to do four things," I said, determined to move forward. "No. 1, they're required to fix your teeth in prison, so get them fixed." Darryl's teeth were yellowed from not having any dental work done in years. "The second thing you do is you take every class they offer you. I don't care if it's cake decorating. When you come out, and they say, 'Darryl Hunt, what can you do?' you can say, 'I can decorate a cake.'

"And read. Read every book you can get your hands on. Educate yourself while you're in prison.

"And the fourth and most important thing -- and the best advice I can give you – is hold on to your good attitude, and keep your head up. Don't ever hang your head as if you're guilty. Always look at the positive side and know that some day this will be over. If not in this life, in the next. Some day the world will know that you are not guilty."

Visiting time came to an end, and I wondered when I would ever see Darryl again.

"I'll try to keep up with you," I said as I rose to leave. "I'll make sure I know where you are."

* * *

Keeping up with Darryl was harder than I thought.

After our last visit in Winston-Salem, he was moved more than 20 times.

Our Christmas cards and letters bounced all over the state. Darryl said he was told that keeping him on the move saved him from other inmates who wanted to kill him, but that he suspected there were other reasons.

"They don't want me to have visitors. It's too much of a hassle for them," he told me.

He also felt that the moves sabotaged his education. It seemed that every time he was about to finish a class – first his GED courses and then college classes -- he was transferred to another facility.

Any time I ran into a former student who knew Darryl, I asked how he was doing. Some were able to offer a crumb or two. Some didn't know any more than I did.

I knew that Mark Rabil had appealed the verdict and was continuing to work on freeing Darryl. There were times I called his office just to hear his voice. I didn't ask for details. I just wanted some reassurance that everything was being done that could be done.

And I prayed. Every day I prayed that God would intervene and that Darryl Hunt would come home.

* * *

The fall after the trial, when school started at Philo, I began telling the Darryl Hunt story to my sixth grade class, and I told it every year until I retired in 1998. I felt that sharing his story with my students accomplished two things. It taught them about the consequences of dropping out of school and keeping bad company. And it kept me connected to Darryl.

I illustrated the story with newspaper articles and pictures about the murder and the trial, but also with stories of Darryl as a sixth grader – a child my students could understand. When I told them about Darryl, the mouse hunter, they understood the importance of what he did because they didn't want mice eating the candy I gave them during Friday afternoon Bingo games.

Near the end of each school year, I asked an aide to come in and stay with my class while I took the black children into another room. I wanted to talk to them alone about the challenges they were about to face in the seventh grade. And the rest of their lives.

My message was simple. While life is not always fair, there are ways to overcome that unfairness.

"You're going to have to work twice as hard as the white children in your class next year," I told the little group huddled around me as if they were about to go onto the football field and we were discussing game strategy. "And you're going to have to make people realize that you are capable. When you grow up, and you and a white person go for a job interview, which one do you think is going to be hired? You've got to realize that now, and you've got to start working really hard.

"If you don't remember anything else, there are two things I want you to remember. First, you are known by the company you keep. Second, don't ever accuse a white person of being prejudiced. If you do, you've lost two ways. If they are prejudice, it makes them more so. If they're not prejudice, you've lost a friend."

Darryl was never far from my mind, no matter where I was or what I was doing.

Once, after hearing a state attorney speak at the Governor's School, I introduced myself as Darryl Hunt's teacher. I told him that I had appeared as a character witness during the trial and asked him what he thought of the case.

"I don't think there was enough evidence," he said. "You have nothing to be concerned about. I think the new trial will prove him innocent."

"Grandma, there's lots worse things than being an old maid," I said. The old woman looked me straight in the eye and shot back, "Name one."

CHAPTER TWELVE

The trial of Darryl Hunt seemed to launch me into one life-changing event after another.

Not long after the trial was over, I heard that I had been named Philo Middle School Teacher of the Year. I felt honored, but the thrill of being recognized for my hard work was dampened by my concern for Darryl.

Everything in my life was affected by the powerlessness I felt in the face of such injustice. I tried to move through the days in the same way I had before the trial, but my steps felt slower and not as light.

Since my divorce from Charles North in 1976, I had been content with my life as a single woman. When I wasn't teaching, I bowled or enjoyed a movie or dinner with a casual date. But my friends and family were never as satisfied with my single status as I was, and they all seemed to be on a mission to get me married again.

I felt like I had been flashed back to my teenage years in the mountains of North Carolina with my grandmother, Laura Cole. Grandma lived near Fleetwood High School, and I slept at her house after playing basketball so nobody had to drive me home late at night.

Every time I went to visit her, she said, "Jo Anne, when are you going to get married?"

Over and over, I told her I had no plans to get married any time soon. I wanted to go to college. Once, I tried to put a stop to the questions with a firm stand.

"Grandma, there's lots worse things than being an old maid," I said.

The old woman looked me straight in the eye and shot back, "Name one."

I was in my 50s and divorced when my friend Big House Gaines took the same approach.

"Jo Anne, when in the world are you going to get married again?" he joked every time he saw me.

My answer was always the same. "One of these days."

"You're wasting your life," was his constant comeback.

Finally, I caved in. "Okay, House, next time you go to recruit basketball players, you recruit me a husband."

After the recruiting season was over, I asked him if he had found a man for me.

"No, Jo Anne, they wanted all your health and dental records, and I didn't have them with me."

* * *

I had been single for 10 years when I met Milton Goetz.

One afternoon, on our way back from Myrtle Beach, my friend Betty Love mentioned her boss. Milt was the manager of information systems at Summit Communications, a Winston-Salem company that owned a couple of radio stations and cable companies.

"Jo Anne, I've got the nicest boss who's just moved here from New York," Betty said. "Would you like to meet him?"

I said I would, and she agreed to arrange a meeting. She showed him my picture, and a few days later, he called and asked me to meet him at the New Market Grill on Stratford Road.

A girlfriend dropped me off in front of the restaurant shortly before 5:30 on a Thursday afternoon, and I stood outside waiting for Milt. Betty had described him to me, so when a tall, good-looking man in a suit and tie walked around the corner looking like he owned the world, I said, "Think you could be picked up?"

He could.

That Saturday, he took me to watch Wake Forest University play Clemson. Wake Forest lost, but I've always believed that game was a turning point in my life.

I sat in the bleachers and suffered as the kicker missed one field goal after another. Finally, with only five minutes left, the coach took him out of the game.

I stood up and shrieked.

"What's the matter?" Milt asked.

"Look at the score," I yelled. "What good will it do to replace that poor kid now? Wake Forest can't win. But if that little boy can make just one field goal, he'll feel a whole lot better than if he sits on the bench thinking, 'I missed every one of them.' That coach just doesn't think about how things affect people."

Milt told me later that it was my compassion for that kicker that won his heart. But it took a while.

After the football game, he called.

"You know, Jo Anne, this dating thing is all new to me," he said. "I think I need to get my life straightened out and take it slow."

We didn't go out together again after that call, but I didn't forget Milton Goetz and his glamorous world. The part of me that was still a little girl from the mountains of North Carolina was charmed by his New York City roots, his prep school education and his management position at Summit Communications.

I knew when his birthday was, so before I left for a middle school conference in Baltimore, I mailed him a birthday card to arrive on November 18.

When I got home, Mother said Milt had called to thank me for the card. "That's nice," I said, but I didn't return his call. I had heard he was seeing the music teacher at Atkins Middle School.

The next month, Milt called again. This time I was home.

"Hey," he said. "This is Milt Goetz."

"Who?" I teased him.

"Milt Goetz."

"Oh, yes. I think I remember you."

"A funny thing happened to me on the way to the Christmas party," he joked.

"What's that?"

"I don't have a date. I know it's late to ask, but will you go with me?"

When he came to pick me up, I could see that he was struggling with what to say after three months.

"My, those are pretty red shoes you're wearing," was all he could come up with. I laughed and stood on tiptoe to kiss him on the cheek.

Milt and I married on February 20, 1988 – within days of his divorce -- and a month after the wedding, Summit Communications was sold to a company in Atlanta. For two months, we lived with the uncertainty of whether Milt was going to have a job or not.

In May, the company moved four Summit Communications people to Atlanta -- the owner, the finance manager, an accountant and Milt.

I knew I had three things to do before I could join Milt -- sell my townhouse, finish the summer session at the Governor's School and see Darryl Hunt.

As I heard the clang of the metal locks behind us,
I thought about what that must sound like if you
knew you were there for the rest of your life.

CHAPTER THIRTEEN

I phoned Mark Rabil to find out where Darryl was being held.

A lot had happened since the last time I saw Mark. In November of 1985, city manager Bill Stuart had issued a report accusing police of procedural errors and sloppy work in the Sykes investigation. In January and February 1986, Jim Daulton, the lead investigator, had been demoted to a dispatcher position because of the way police lineups had been conducted; two supervisors had been suspended; and the chief had been reprimanded. Don Tisdale had lost the Democratic primary to Warren Sparrow.

The next year, Sammy and Darryl had been indicted for the September 1983 murder of Arthur Wilson, a 57-year-old black man who had spent several hours with them in a drink house in Winston-Salem the night he was killed.

Merritt Drayton, in custody in April 1986 and charged with his girlfriend's death, said he had been with Sammy and Darryl that night and saw them kill Wilson. Darryl admitted to being at the drink house but said he left before Sammy did and that Wilson was alive when he left.

In October 1986, Sammy Mitchell had been convicted and sentenced to 50 years in prison for the murder of Arthur Wilson.

In September 1987, Darryl had been convicted of second-degree murder and sentenced to 40 years.

I was not surprised when Mark told me he had not represented Darryl in the Wilson case. I knew he had spent thousands of hours and was still recovering financially from the Sykes trial.

We talked about what the Wilson conviction might have done to Darryl's chances.

"You know, Jo Anne, this Wilson case provides the perfect comeback to the city manager's report," Mark said. "During the Sykes trial, people said if it had been a drink house murder, they would have had no doubt that Darryl did it. Now they can say 'Even if he didn't do the Sykes murder, he did this.' It may help destroy any supporters we have who may be on the fence."

One crumb of good news Mark was able to offer me was that Johnny Gray had been convicted of murder in the 1987 death of Willis Mabe. A motion had been filed for a new trial in the Sykes case, based on an affidavit from Johnny's girlfriend Lisa McBride in which she said Gray admitted killing Sykes.

Still, as I listened to Mark's voice on the phone, I thought he sounded like he was at the bottom of a very deep, black hole.

I could only imagine what Darryl felt like.

* * *

The skies were slate gray and just beginning to spit rain on the morning Milt and I drove to visit Darryl at the Piedmont Correctional Institute in Salisbury. My mood matched the weather.

I worried about whether my name had gotten on the visiting list. About whether Milt's name would be on the list with mine. What if they won't let him go in with me? What if Darryl has been moved and isn't even there?

What will he look like? Has he changed?

I knew that Milt had a lot of things on his mind concerning his move to Atlanta and that he didn't really want to make the trip with me. But he had agreed to go, and Milt Goetz was a man of his word.

Milt was born in Brooklyn, New York and moved to Winston-Salem from Schenectady in 1984. I knew he couldn't possibly understand my life, beginning with the one-room schoolhouse in Oval, North Carolina. He had never grown up with an old black man who refused to eat at the same table with him or let his hands touch the cornbread they shared. He had never raced through the night with a sick black friend on the front seat beside him and a pickup truck with two white boys on his rear bumper.

And he would never know the stigma a white woman faces when she stands up for a black man in the rural south.

"How do you know Darryl Hunt is innocent?" Milt asked.

"It's a gut feeling," I said. "Very few people have spent as much time with Darryl as I did as his teacher. I knew his heart when he was 12 years old, and I don't think hearts change."

"How about if the kid starts doing drugs?"

"Maybe. But Darryl wasn't doing drugs."

"How do you know?"

"He told me."

* * *

Our drive down the interstate seemed endless. After passing through a heavily wooded area, the road curved and suddenly we faced the Piedmont Correctional Institute.

The seven-story building was surrounded by a tall chain length fence topped by razor wire. Guards stood in the towers with rifles.

I was glad Milt had remembered to bring an umbrella as we made the long dash in the rain from the parking lot to the front door. We shook ourselves off and signed in at the office. I saw only one other name on Darryl's visitor's list -- Mark Rabil.

As we stood waiting, I noticed a smell like a dirty, wet rag mop that has been used to clean up cigarette butts. And beans cooking.

Milt and I left wallet and purse with the prison personnel and were ushered down a hall up to a sliding glass door. The door opened and we walked through a glass vestibule toward a second glass door. I sensed that our every move was being observed by security as we made our way through this passageway like boats passing through a lock.

As I heard the heavy clang behind us, I thought about what that must sound like if you knew you were there for the rest of your life.

A guard escorted us to a visiting room that looked and smelled like many teachers' break rooms I had seen in the past. Orange chairs that were as hard as their color was bright and had been sat in one too many times. Tables with the veneer starting to peel off in places where people had leaned their elbows. A line of drink machines stood in one corner like metal sentries. Stale cigarette smoke and cheap perfume hung heavy in the room.

I moved as close to Milt as our separate seats would allow and waited. As the minutes ticked by, I wondered what was taking so long. I wondered how much prison would have changed Darryl. Whether the gentleness that survived life on the streets and the local jail had finally been stolen from him by the prison guards and his fellow inmates. People who treated him like a murderer. A black man who had killed a white woman.

As soon as Darryl walked in the room, I knew I had nothing to worry about.

Darryl Hunt wore the prison uniform of kaki pants and jacket and white tee shirt like a second skin, but the smile was the same one that touched my heart at Mebane Elementary School.

"You've had your teeth fixed," I said as I pulled out of our hug.

"Yes, ma'am."

"And look at you. You look great. Where did you get those muscles?"

"Yes, ma'am. Guess I have bulked up some since I last saw you. Been lifting weights and playing some basketball."

I realized that Milt was standing behind me, not knowing what to say or do.

"Darryl, this is my husband Milt Goetz."

"Nice to meet you, sir, but she'll always be Ms. North to me." We all laughed, relieved by the icebreaker. We sat at the table, Milt and me on one side, facing Darryl on the other.

Darryl told me that he had been taking classes to get his GED and that he had converted to Islam on November 5, 1985.

"The commitment was something I felt would help me be disciplined," he explained. "I've felt closer to God. You know, Ms. North, in Islam, you've got to pray five times a day. That keeps me focused and conscious."

He said he had read the biography of Malcolm X and had wanted to know more about his religion and what had made him change. Darryl said he started to study the Quran.

"I felt like it fitted me," he said.

"I'm grateful for anything that helps you get through this until we can get you out. I still believe the witnesses at your trial weren't credible. Someday, Darryl, you'll be free."

I didn't know how long we'd been there when the guard said it was time for Darryl to leave us. I wasn't ready to say good-bye. Atlanta seemed worlds away, and I wasn't sure when I'd see him again.

"Darryl, you take care of yourself," I said and kissed his cheek. "Take care of your body and your mind. They're all you've got now. Everybody else has control of the rest of your comings and goings, but they can't control your mind."

"Yes, ma'am," he said and moved away from me. He stopped and turned around before he got to the door and walked back. "Guess where I'm working, Ms. North."

"Where?"

"In the kitchen. I learned how to decorate a cake."

* * *

I was able to hold the tears back until Darryl was out of the room. Milt handed me his handkerchief and patted me on the shoulder.

"Thanks for coming," I said.

"I'm glad I came," were the first words out of Milt's mouth since he'd walked in the prison doors. I looked into his eyes and saw something that hadn't been there before the visit. I saw that he believed.

As Milt and I walked out the door, I stopped in front of the guard I had noticed glaring at me throughout the entire visit.

"I guess you wonder what a white woman is doing visiting Darryl Hunt," I said.

The man continued to glare.

"Well, I'm going to tell you. I was Darryl's teacher 10 years ago, and I went to court for him because I know that he could not have murdered anybody. I was committed to him then, and I'm committed to him now."

"Really? You're that convinced, are you?"

"Yes, sir, I am."

As I watched, the man's stone face softened.

"Well, ma'am, I respect you for doing that," he said. "I've been doing this for a long time, and I don't know very many people who would have done what you did."

"What hope did Deborah Sykes cling to then? Where
was the judge and where was the jury? When
life's blood ran on the grass?" (second trial, closing
argument by special prosecutor, Dean Bowman)

CHAPTER FOURTEEN

I kept up with news of Darryl through Mark Rabil and my sister, Rita, who fed me bits and pieces from the local media, but my heartstrings felt stretched much too thin by the distance between Atlanta and Winston-Salem.

Many times my letters to Darryl were returned unopened, and I never knew why. To continue writing seemed like a waste of time, and there were months when I gave up my efforts to communicate. When I couldn't stand the feeling of isolation from him a minute longer, I picked up pen and paper and tried one more time.

My plan had been to retire from teaching after Milt and I left Winston-Salem. I had lined up a job with a publishing company, but changed my mind during the July break from Governor's School.

I was flying to Atlanta to be with Milt and somewhere over South Carolina, the strong conviction hit me that I couldn't leave my children.

"I can't help Darryl now, but maybe I can help somebody else," I heard my inner voice say. "Maybe there's another Darryl in Atlanta who needs me."

As soon as I got home, the first words out of my mouth to Milt were, "I'm going back to teaching."

Milt looked like he had been hit over the head with a sledgehammer.

"Jo Anne, you can't do that," he said. "You've put so much work into getting this new job. You can't back out now."

"Oh, yes, I can," I said, and I did.

After the courts had ordered school integration, many of the new teachers sent to formerly all-black schools in south DeKalb County lasted a year and then quit. In an effort to remedy the problem, the school board had instituted a teacher lottery designed to fill those teaching positions with teachers who had long-term experience.

Names of teachers with at least 20 years in the classroom were drawn from a hat and sent to the schools that needed them. The plan failed when many of the teachers chosen decided to retire rather than accept those assignments.

Milt's secretary told me about the teacher shortage, and I called the school administration office and asked for an interview with the personnel director.

"He's not available," the receptionist said.

"What time does he go to lunch?"

I was met with total silence.

"Does he go to lunch?" I asked again.

"Well, he usually goes around noon," the woman stammered.

"I'll be there," I said and hung up.

I drove over to the man's office and sat outside his door with my 31 years of experience, ready and willing to do what others wouldn't. When he opened his door and came out to leave for lunch, I stood up and told him why I was there.

"Where do you want to teach?" he asked.

"I've taught in all-white schools, and I've taught in integrated schools," I said. "I understand you have some all-black classes that need teachers, and that's where I want to go."

"Go on over to McNair Junior High School. It's all-black. Check it out and come back and tell me what you think."

I did what I was told, even though the only thing I could check out was an empty school building since everybody was on summer break. I wasn't sure what I would find in another month when school started again, but I took the job.

* * *

The pace of life in Atlanta was much faster than it had been in Winston-Salem and involved a 64-mile round trip to and from school each day. My daily routine was to leave my home in Dunwoody, a neighborhood in the north side of the city, at 6 a.m. and drive the beltway to the south end of Atlanta. Each day, I taught four social studies classes with a total of 115 students.

I tried to leave school early enough so that I arrived at Spaghetti Junction before 5 p.m. If I weren't able to get away in time, traffic became so backed up at that huge interstate crossing that I felt like I was stuck in a gigantic parking lot.

There were many days when I stayed after school to attend extra-curricular activities, including working with the student government as a faculty advisor. Getting home late and having to grade 115 papers became more and more of a challenge for me as I hit my 60s.

But I loved a challenge and faced it head on. I drove the miles, faced the mounting discipline problems and was rewarded by being named Teacher of the Year at McNair in 1994. I spent the next year at Taylor Road Middle School in Fulton County and then returned to DeKalb County for two years at Henderson Middle School before I retired.

During the summers, I returned to Winston-Salem to work at the Governor's School. I had hoped that being in North Carolina would mean I could see Darryl more often, but my work schedule prevented those visits.

I always found time to pray.

* * *

1989 was a big year for Darryl Hunt.

In May I heard from Mark that the N. C. Supreme Court had overturned the Sykes conviction because Tisdale had introduced statements made by Margaret Crawford after she denied them. My heart was in North Carolina, rejoicing with Darryl.

Six months later, the court overturned his Wilson conviction because the trial judge had given the jury flawed instructions about the law.

In November, Mark called to tell me that Darryl had gotten out of prison on a $50,000 bond raised by the National Council of Churches, using Larry Little's house as collateral. I smiled when I heard that Darryl was taking classes at Winston-Salem State University and that he had gotten a job in the cafeteria at Forsyth County's Reynolds Health Center.

Mark told me that Warren Sparrow, the new District Attorney, was not going to prosecute the retrial because two assistants in his office –Mark's brother, Vince Rabil, and Todd Burke -- had been involved in Darryl's defense during the first Sykes trial. Dean Bowman, the Surry County District Attorney, and James Yeatts had been assigned to the case as special prosecutors.

During his days as a Black Panther, Larry Little had met James Ferguson, a star civil-rights lawyer from Charlotte who had defended the Wilmington 10 during their firebombing trial. Larry asked him and his partner Adam Stein to represent Darryl in the second Sykes trial, and they agreed to take the case. The

Darryl Hunt Defense Fund, which continued to grow from the outpouring of local support, was to pay their legal fees.

Mark also told me that Darryl was living with Khalid Griggs, Imam of the Community Mosque of Winston-Salem. I got his phone number and called.

"How are you feeling about the retrial?" I asked Darryl when he came to the phone.

"Ms. North, I really think this one will clear me."

"What does Mark think?"

"I think he feels the same way."

But Darryl was feeling positive about more than a new trial. He had met Griggs' step-daughter, April Clark, a student at Winston-Salem State University, who lived at home with her 2-year-old daughter. She had a boyfriend at the time, but that didn't stop her from being kind to Darryl.

I could hear a smile in his voice when he talked about their friendship and felt grateful he had something to smile about.

"It's always good to have someone special in your life," I said. "Enjoy her."

* * *

When I called Mark in the late spring of 1990, he said that Darryl's defense team had filed a motion to move the retrial to another urban county but had had no luck.

There had been no room on the court calendar in Raleigh, Durham or Fayetteville. Judge Forrest Ferrell, who lived in Catawba County, moved the trial to Newton, a small town near Hickory. It was there that Darryl's defense attorneys had won with an all-white jury in the Wilson retrial.

But the Wilson story was very different from the Sykes'. Black men killing another black man was world's apart from a black man killing a white woman.

* * *

Darryl's retrial in the Sykes murder began in September 1990. The jury was all white and the State's case relied on eyewitness testimony again.

I kept the phone lines hot between Mark Rabil's office and Atlanta during the trial.

The State called some of the same witnesses: Ferguson argued that Thomas Murphy had changed his statements, first saying there were two men, then four.

He argued that Johnny Gray was an unreliable witness because he was in prison for murder.

Weaver had said in the first trial he saw Darryl in the lobby. In the retrial, he said he saw Sammy and Darryl on the street.

The State called Margaret Crawford again and Ferguson exposed her lies.

She was living in Atlanta when the detectives finally caught up with her before the retrial. This time when they questioned her, she said Darryl spent the night of August 9 with her but was gone when she got up the next morning. She said he had blood on his hands when he returned, and that when she and Darryl saw the Crime Stoppers report, he told her that he and Sammy Mitchell had tried to rob Sykes and that Sammy had killed her.

Crawford said she denied her statements in the first trial because she was afraid of Sammy Mitchell.

The State also called some new faces. Two prison inmate snitches said Darryl confessed to the crime while in prison. Ferguson discredited the first one, Jesse M. Moore, as a racist who believed that blacks got preferential treatment in prison, and the second, Donald Haigy, with testimony by his brother who called him a liar. A third inmate said Darryl didn't confess.

Another new witness, Debra Davis, said she saw Darryl and Sammy near Crystal Towers on August 10, but Ferguson argued

---

[8] The Chronicle, "Let the Record Speak for Itself," June 26, 1997.

that she was on probation for welfare fraud and wanted to gain favor with the police.

Kevey Coleman had told SBI investigators that he saw a white woman with two black men near the scene of the crime. One was lighter skinned and wore a beard; he couldn't identify the other man. Ferguson argued that Coleman was nearsighted and not wearing his contact lenses on August 10.

Another new witness was Ed Reese, who said he saw Mitchell near Crystal Towers about 7 a.m. on August 10. That didn't look good for Darryl, who had said for five years that he was with Mitchell all that morning.

Statements by Coleman and Reese had led to Sammy Mitchell's indictment in January 1990 on a charge of murder in Sykes' death.

During the retrial, Ferguson didn't call Darryl to the stand because he was afraid his testimony would lead to doubts about his alibi. In closing statements, Yeatts attacked that alibi, using Cynthia McKey's testimony.

During the first trial, McKey had said that Darryl and Sammy were at her house at 7 a.m. August 10. She said she knew what time it was because she got up to take her children to school. When detectives remembered that school didn't start in August in 1984 and questioned her about it, she admitted to lying and said that Darryl and Sammy were gone when she woke up.

Yeatts also argued that there was more than one attacker, maybe Johnnny Gray, maybe someone else.

The defense spent two days on closing arguments, trying to show that each witness had been pushed into making the identifications.

"I think we have to call these facts as they are," Ferguson said. "And I say to you right now, with no qualms at all, that what I have heard from the prosecution is a case of extraordinarily low quality, and the State has tried to make up in quantity what it lacks in quality. But I have to say to you that a pile of trash does not get better as it gets bigger. It simply makes it more difficult to sift through to see if there's anything of value."

Bowman countered Ferguson's sarcastic, intellectual argument with a passionate, graphic and heartbreaking portrayal of Deborah Sykes' death.

"She put on this light blouse here when she got up to go to work," he said, holding up the sleeveless knit blouse caked with mud and blood.

"Maybe she was thinking of having a baby," he said, as some of the jurors began to cry.

"And what was she thinking when this man right over here, this Darryl Eugene Hunt, what was she thinking when he pinned her down to the ground, held her arms up and he slashed her and he slashed her and he slashed her and he slashed her some more, just like he was butchering some animal?

"Finally, what was Deborah Sykes thinking when this man right over here, this real person Deborah Sykes, what was she thinking when he spread those legs apart, and he crawled down inside her, and he raped and ravaged her and deposited some thick yellow sickening fluid in her body?

"What hope did Deborah Sykes cling to then? Where was the judge and where was the jury? When life's blood ran on the grass?" [7]

The jury deliberated less than two hours, and Darryl was found guilty of first-degree murder, robbery, kidnapping, sexual assault and rape and sentenced again to life in prison.

---

[7] Winston-Salem Journal, November 21, 2003, Phoebe Zerwick's eight-part series "Murder, Race, Justice."

"The whole world needs to know about this," Larry
Little said. "If you allow people to do this, you
kill your own soul. We've got to keep trying."

CHAPTER FIFTEEN

The retrial and its unhappy outcome became the next chapter in the Darryl Hunt story I told my school children in Atlanta.

The reaction in the all-black classroom where I taught was different than it had been in Winston-Salem. I was the minority, and the children felt safety in their numbers. I remember the first time I told the tragic story, and a black eighth-grader named Jerome raised his hand at the end.

"Ms. Goetz," he said in a pre-adolescent squeak, "are you mixed?"

I was glad I was sitting down at the time. I had never been asked that question before, and it threw me off balance.

"I'm sorry, would you ask that question again. I'm not sure I heard you right." I said, stalling for time.

"Are you mixed?" he asked again with the naked honesty that only children possess.

I stood up and walked over to his seat and looked down at him. I smiled and patted him on the back. "Of course, I am," I said. "Just like everybody else. You know, only dogs and horses are purebred and have papers to show their bloodline."

The class laughed and went back to their work.

I wondered why none of my students in North Carolina had ever asked the question. I wondered if people in the courtroom had puzzled over the issue. If the same thought had crossed the mind of the sheriff's deputy in Salisbury.

I never knew the answer as to why others hadn't asked, but as a result of Jerome's bravery in Atlanta, I felt a kinship to the group of children who had honored me with the suggestion that part of me was like them.

* * *

Darryl's defense team changed after the second Sykes trial.

Mark told me the story.

Since part of the appeal for a third trial related to Bowman's closing argument -- which Ferguson had let him make without objection -- someone else needed to argue that Darryl deserved a retrial.

Ben Dowling-Sendor, from the state's appellate defender's office, was appointed to represent Darryl in the appeal, and Mark and a private investigator, Richard McGough, continued to search for new evidence. District Attorney Warren Sparrow had lost the general election a month after the second trial, and his replacement, Tom Keith, assigned his lead assistant Eric Saunders to represent the State.

Darryl's attorneys focused on finding new witnesses and trying to get the complete 1986 State Bureau of Investigation report they had requested before the first trial. Their work started a new round of hearings, with the North Carolina Supreme Court asking Judge Metzer Morgan of Forsyth Superior Court to hear testimony from the new witnesses and to review the six-volume SBI report.

Hearings began in June 1993, with testimony that Johnny Gray had confessed to his own role in the murder and rape of

Deborah Sykes. At this point, Mark and Ferguson were appointed to represent Darryl in the hearings.

The big development came when Mark, Sendor and McGough read about a case of a death-row inmate in Maryland. Kirk Bloodsworth had been cleared after DNA testing eliminated him as the source of a semen stain on the victim's panties. He was the first person in the nation convicted in a death penalty case to be exonerated by DNA testing.

Darryl agreed to be tested, but Saunders opposed the motion, saying the new polymerase chain reaction, or PCR, tests weren't reliable. In the late 1980s, forensic scientists had perfected the new technology that allowed them to compare DNA from very small or even degraded samples, using enzymes and other chemicals to extract DNA from blood or human tissue and copy it many times so it could be compared.

In April 1994, Judge Morgan ordered DNA testing and, finally, in September of that year, Darryl gave blood for the test – 10 years after his arrest in the Sykes murder. LabCorp in Research Triangle Park finished the test in October 1994.

The DNA in the semen didn't match Darryl's. It was the first physical evidence in the case, and it contradicted all the testimony that he was involved.

Finally, it's over, I thought. It was just a nightmare.

But Saunders didn't give up. He argued that Darryl could be guilty of murder even if he hadn't raped Sykes.

He had Sammy Mitchell's, Johnny Gray's and Doug Sykes' DNA tested. On November 3, four days before the hearing on the DNA, the report came back showing that none of them matched.

Keith opposed Darryl's release and a new trial, arguing that it was possible that somebody else raped Sykes, or that Darryl raped her without ejaculating.

At the DNA hearing, Saunders questioned whether the sample had been tampered with. Richard Guerrieri, a forensic scientist with LabCorp testified that it was a valid test and that there was no evidence of tampering.

Judge Morgan called a three-day recess at the end of the 1994 DNA hearing. When court reconvened, he ruled that the new evidence would not have made enough of a difference that a jury might have rendered a different verdict. Darryl could have raped her and not ejaculated or not raped her but killed her. Witnesses had said he was at the scene.

Mark said he had seen two warning signs that the final injustice was about to happen.

First, Darryl had always worn a tie and belt in all the other hearings, but when he walked into the courtroom that day, he wore neither and was upset that they had been taken away from him. Mark understood this as a sign that the sheriff's deputies knew something was about to be said that might lead to his hurting himself or someone else.

Second, the judge began by warning that anybody who couldn't sit quietly through the reading of the ruling should leave before he began. Everybody remained seated, but one supporter burst out with words about the "corrupt court," and a sheriff's deputy ordered him from the courtroom.

Later, Darryl told Mark that he had become immune to being discarded.

I didn't feel immune and wondered what I would have done had I been there. Somebody's been paid off, I thought. Darryl's been set up again, and there's nothing I can do about it.

After the hearing, Sendor told reporters that Darryl had been "judicially lynched." He did the only thing that he could do -- appeal. He argued that Morgan's ruling might have made sense if the DNA evidence had not also excluded the other suspects in the case. But, if neither Darryl, nor Mitchell nor Gray had raped Sykes, who did? An unidentified fourth person?

None of the witnesses who claimed to have seen Darryl and Sammy said they saw another person.

The North Carolina Supreme Court affirmed Morgan's decision in December 1994 in a 4-3 decision. The majority opinion failed to mention the DNA evidence and ruled that the 1990 trial was error-free.

Mark told me that when he and Larry Little called Darryl in prison to break the news to him, he thanked them for what they had done. But the train had finally hit him. The phone went dead.

"The whole world needs to know about this," Larry had said. "If you allow people to do this, you kill your own soul. We've got to keep trying."

* * *

My sister Rita mailed me a videotape of a WXII Channel 12 interview with Darryl in the Marion Correctional Center that winter.

Watching the footage in Atlanta, I saw that Darryl and Mark had changed a lot since I saw them last. Darryl looked like he had been lifting weights. Mark's hair had thinned and his beard had flecks of silver in it, but his eyes still burned with the passion of his youth.

I recognized the slow, low-pitched voice and the gentle way of speaking as Darryl talked to reporter Cameron Kent.

"I haven't done anything, but I'm here. Why me?" Darryl said. He admitted drinking a lot during 1984 but said he never did marijuana, cocaine or other drugs or "robbed people or beat people up."

"I didn't do it," he said, looking Cameron Kent in the eye.

Mark's partner, Gordon Jenkins told of meeting with Darryl about the DNA testing and quoted him as saying, "You can do any test any time, and it will never prove I did it because I wasn't even there."

Cameron Kent asked Darryl why he didn't show any emotion during the second trial when he was found guilty again and sentenced to life.

"It was a given," Darryl said. "We knew what we were going to get. It was no surprise."

"Why didn't you pound your fist on the table and rant and rave?"

"I'm not that way. I'm not a violent person."

Later in the interview, Kent asked Darryl why he didn't accept the plea bargain offered him during the Wilson trial. An offer that would have released him from jail with five years served for the combined Wilson and Sykes conviction if he had pled guilty to both.

Darryl could have walked away at that time a free man. A healthy 24-year-old man with the rest of his life ahead of him – with April waiting on the other side of the bars -- and still he refused.

My heart filled with pride as I watched Darryl Hunt look Cameron Kent in the eye and answer the question.

"Because I didn't do nothing," Darryl said. "I don't believe if you did not commit a crime – why admit something you didn't do. I couldn't live with myself. And, it wouldn't be over. I'll still be looked at as a person who committed a crime I didn't do, and the person who did it is still out there."

* * *

I wrote to Darryl while he was there in Marion, filling him in on what I was doing and offering a little news about his fellow students in Winston-Salem.

Dear Darryl, I wrote,

Even though it has been a while since we have communicated, I have never quit praying for you and telling my students your story.

My family keeps me informed as to your status, and I hear from Mark the latest news.

I am still teaching. You would think I would tire of it, but I never do. I still love working with kids.

When I moved to Atlanta, I taught eighth grade social studies in an all-black junior high school. I was there five years and stress got to me, so I took a year off and had foot surgery and worked for the Olympics.

I am still doing the Governor's School at Salem College. This is my 31st summer.

Lisa Jackson worked in the dining hall for a while, but her mother is very ill and she can't work right now.

Lisa told me that Wayne Baskins is still around, also Percy Caruthers and Paul Williams.

It is heartening to know where you are. Surely hope you still have your positive attitude because God makes no mistakes, and He will take care of you.

Love,
Ms. North (Goetz)

*Darryl's eyes roamed the room and seemed
to focus on things I couldn't see.*

CHAPTER SIXTEEN

Milt and I retired in 1998 and moved back to Winston-Salem the next year.

As soon as my work at the Governor's School was over that fall, I headed for Salisbury to visit Darryl.

The weather was rainy, like it had been during my visit 10 years before, but this time I didn't have Milt there to share the umbrella. Although I missed my husband's company, I understood that he felt like a fifth wheel, and I didn't push him to go with me. I was not facing the unknown this time and felt more confident as I set off on the hour's drive to Salisbury.

Piedmont Correctional Institute hadn't changed much during my absence. Perhaps a few more scuff marks on the walls and another layer of cigarette smoke. As I sat waiting for Darryl, I wondered what the decade behind prison walls had done to him.

It seemed like hours passed as I sat waiting, listening to the other inmates and their visitors around me. Whispers. Laughter. Crying. A steady drone of voices filled the space like bees in a hive.

Even though I had confirmed that Darryl was in Salisbury, I worried that something had gone wrong. That he'd been moved again. That I was going to be given some other reason why I couldn't see Darryl.

When the guard finally escorted him into the visiting room, I wasn't entirely prepared for what I saw. The videotape of the interview with Cameron Kent in Marion hadn't been the flesh and bones that stood in front of me.

Darryl wore a Muslim prayer cap called a "kufi" and, as I looked at it for the first time, I felt as though I were facing a stranger. A foreigner. But as soon as my eyes moved from the kufi to the face beneath it, I knew I was looking at my Darryl.

But he wasn't the same man I had said goodbye to in this same room 10 years before. His body seemed to have shrunk into itself, and his eyes had lost some of their boyish light. They roamed the room and seemed to focus on things I couldn't see.

Darryl had looked stunned when he walked into the room and found me instead of April. I was the last person he was expecting since he didn't know I had moved back to North Carolina.

We hugged and then he stood back to look at me.

"You look great, Ms. North," he said. "You haven't changed since Mebane."

I laughed and accepted the compliment. All my former students said those same words when they saw me, despite the 20 years and the switch from a blond to a redhead. I knew what they meant. It wasn't the hair color, added weight or wrinkles that my students looked at when we were reunited. They saw something much deeper – my love.

I brought Darryl up to date on Milt's and my retirement, our move back to Winston-Salem, my work on the school bond referendum and news of his former classmates I had seen around town.

Darryl sat and looked at me as attentively as he had in the sixth grade. I had been afraid that the mention of people he knew who were free might sadden him, but he seemed to appreciate word from Winston like a cool drink of water.

The realization hit me in the face. Darryl Hunt had accepted that he was locked up for something he didn't do. Locked up for life.

"You look like you've lost some weight," I said, trying to make conversation. "What's going on?"

"Things have changed," he said. "I was lifting weights and playing basketball before, but not now."

I asked Darryl what he meant and heard stories I would never have believed if anybody but Darryl had told them. I didn't want to believe that he feared for his life.

The threats had begun even before he left the jail in Winston-Salem. After the sentencing, he had been returned to what was called "the hole," a tiny windowless room with no ventilation. As the guards left, they told him that the last "nigger" who had been there had been found hanging from the bars. More than once, he found a note left on his bed, "Nigger, don't go to sleep. We're going to get you."

After he had been transferred to the prison system, Darryl had been warned by an inmate named "T. C." about a plot to kill him.

T. C. had heard guards talking about assigning Darryl to grease pit duty and then shooting him as he crossed the road to empty the grease in the woods, saying he was trying to escape.

Darryl didn't believe T.C. until the next day when a guard approached him in the chow hall and told him he had grease pit duty. Darryl argued that his life sentence meant he wasn't allowed outside the fence and refused the assignment. As a result of his disobedience to a direct order, he spent the next two months locked up in yet another hole.

Solitary confinement in a tiny cell with no windows was tough for a man with energy to burn.

At every prison camp, he heard rumors of contracts put on his life by skinheads, a branch of the KKK that wanted to see justice done to the man who had raped and murdered a "white rose."

Guards promised drugs for the murder of Darryl Hunt, and he realized that if he wanted to live, he could never go anywhere by himself. No private showers. No sleep unless someone he trusted was willing to stay awake and watch so that he could live to see another sunrise through the steel bars.

I hated the feeling of helplessness in the face of such terror and tried to change the subject.

"Are you reading?"

"Not much. All they allow me is some old books they've got here that were probably written in the '30s."

"Can I bring you some books?"

"No, ma'am. You can't bring me nothing."

I gritted my teeth. I had heard that Darryl had been careful not to cause trouble while he was in prison. I remembered the security guard I had met at Governor's School. The man had worked at the prison in Salisbury and knew Darryl.

"Darryl Hunt is an exemplary inmate," he had said. "He never causes any problems."

I knew I should follow Darryl's lead, but I had a hard time letting go of the idea that I could get Darryl some books. He had written in a letter that he had completed his GED and was working on college credits. I knew that completing his education could be his key to finding a good job when he got out.

I tried to change the subject.

"Remember *The Jack Tales* I used to read to you at Mebane?"

Darryl's face lit up at the mention of Richard Chase's collection of folktales.

"Maybe one day I can read them to my children," he said.

I smiled, but I didn't know what to say. The hope of Darryl ever getting out of prison and having children seemed slim.

"I think they're going to let me get married," he surprised me by saying.

"That's wonderful, Darryl. You must have been behaving yourself, or they wouldn't let you do that. I'm proud of you."

"Yes, ma'am," Darryl said, beaming like we were back at Mebane and I had just handed him a gold star. Then I saw a cloud seem to pass over his face.

"Imam Griggs and the chaplain told April and me we shouldn't bother since I may be here the rest of my life," he said.

"What does April think?"

"She says if we can't be together in this life, we'll be together in the next."

* * *

I was glad to be back in Winston-Salem, for more reasons than one. I enjoyed being part of family gatherings again and became a regular in my old bowling league.

But I couldn't stay away from teaching.

I had heard that Forsyth County had begun a program in which retired educators mentored first- and second-year teachers. I figured if I could mentor at the predominantly black Atkins Middle School, I could pass along some of the lessons I had learned.

I filled out an application -- with the stipulation that I work with Atkins teachers -- and was accepted.

The first year, I worked with nine teachers at Atkins. That number grew to 11 the next year. My mentoring took me to the Kennedy Learning Center, where Khalid Griggs worked as the director of a special program called "Millennium Academy." Each time I was on campus, I asked him about Darryl.

During my third year in the program, I worked at three schools – Philo Middle School, Middle School Academy and Latham Elementary School -- mentoring 17 teachers – two more than the state recommendation of 15.

But in the midst of this three-ring circus of activity, Darryl's face was always in the center ring.

Dr. Jack Noffsinger called one day and said he had a minister friend he wanted me to meet. Rev. Rayford Thompson, Dr. Jack and I met at the K&W for lunch and talked about Darryl.

Thompson had published an article in *The Chronicle* a couple of years earlier,[8] in which he wrote about his tenant, Johnny Gray. Gray had gotten behind on his rent and promised to pay his landlord from money he was going to get from the police for his help in a murder case.

Thompson had written that he didn't know what Gray was talking about until another tenant, Ronald Wiles, identified it as the Sykes case. Gray had told Wiles he had been too far away to identify the attacker as white or black, male or female and that he just wanted to get the money.

Both Thompson and Wiles had signed statements discrediting Gray as a witness.

I felt renewed with hope.

* * *

The year 2000 began a roller coaster of emotions for Darryl and those who cared about him.

Once again, Mark Rabil shared the news of what was going on in the court system.

In February, the 4th U. S. Circuit Court of Appeals turned down his appeal for a new trial.

More than 100 people, including two busloads of students from WSSU, had attended the hearing at the federal courthouse in Richmond. The judges had asked Mark if the DNA results could clear Hunt, despite the fact that several witnesses had said they saw him at the murder scene.

Mark had argued that DNA evidence proved Darryl didn't rape Sykes and negated the theory presented by prosecutors at the

---

[8] The Chronicle, "Let the Record Speak for Itself," June 26, 1997.

second trial that Darryl, Sammy Mitchell and a third man raped and killed her. Mark also said that prosecutors failed to turn over almost 3,000 pages of evidence that contradicted testimony.

In June, Mark filed a petition with the U.S. Supreme Court to grant a third trial. During its October term, the Court affirmed Morgan's ruling and denied another trial.

With each piece of news, I lost another thread of hope.

In September, I received a card from Darryl. The picture on the front showed an open Bible, white lace gloves and a teacup with a silver spoon.

Dear Ms. Goetz, he wrote,

> *I pray my card will find you and your beloved family in the very best of health and spirits. I must apologize for taking so long to write. As you may know, things haven't been going too well with me. However, I have not given up. I believe strongly that God will bring about justice for me.*
>
> *Take care, may God continue to bless, guide and protect you and the family.*
>
> *Sincerely,*
> *Darryl*

I saved the card and savored the words over and over, thankful to hear from him. As a teacher, I noticed Darryl's good penmanship and correct grammar. As his friend, I marveled at the way he had been able to hold on to such a strong faith.

I wondered whether I could have written the same words had I been the one behind bars and realized that somewhere in the past 15 years, Darryl had become the teacher and I the student.

* * *

On October 17, 2000, Darryl and April were married by the prison chaplain at Piedmont Correctional Institution in Salisbury.

Their mutual friend, Nelson Malloy, was the only other person present.

That following December, Mark filed a clemency petition with Gov. Jim Hunt, but the governor left office the next year without reviewing the case. Mike Easley became the next governor of North Carolina.

I didn't hold out much hope that Darryl's case would fare any better with him since Easley had been the attorney general who had defended the State's prosecution of Darryl during the appeal process.

* * *

I received another letter from Darryl in April 2002.

Dear Ms. North, he wrote,

I pray my letter will find you and your beloved family in the very best of health and spirits.

As for myself, I'm doing okay under the circumstances. My faith is strong. God willing, one day this injustice will be over.

Ms. North, as you know, I am married and one of my stepchildren has been having a lot of problems in school. He's been diagnosed with A.D.D. The school system has not done anything to help him. Some weeks he does good in school. Then when he has a bad day, their only solution is to suspend him from school. We're at a complete loss as to what we can do. I told my wife I'm going to write the one person that helped me through my problems in school and ask for her help again. God willing, you can help our son like you helped me. He is in the 4th grade. Around the same age I was when you blessed me with your love. I see in him the same problems I was having with school. Scared and not knowing how to *express my feelings. Afraid of not being smart. For instance, one day at school the teacher had other children grading each other's papers. When one of the kids made a joke out of the fact that my stepson had some answers wrong, he didn't know how to respond and in the end was suspended from school.*

Ms. North, any help you can give this kid will be greatly appreciated.

Thank you. I know with your help, my stepson will become a better student.

Sincerely,
Darryl

I called April Hunt immediately. I called several times, but only spoke to her daughter. Each time, I left my phone number and a request for a return call. When she didn't call me back, I trusted that the boy had gotten help elsewhere.

And I kept praying for his step-father.

"It's finally happened, Jo Anne," Rita said.
"They released Darryl Hunt yesterday."

CHAPTER SEVENTEEN

I n April 2003, Mark obtained a court order from Superior Court Judge Anderson Cromer for the state crime lab to compare the DNA evidence against 40,000 DNA profiles of convicted violent felons and more than 1.5 million nationwide profiles.

That spring, Phoebe Zerwick, an investigative reporter with the *Winston-Salem Journal,* began a nine-month review of more than 30,000 case-related documents. Beginning on November 16, 2003, her eight-part series, "Murder, Race, Justice: The State vs. Darryl Hunt" exposed shocking inconsistencies in the case.

Things began to happen.

Mark called the state crime lab. Nothing had been done since the judge issued his order in April. "We've already told you the DNA didn't match Darryl Hunt," he was told.

"We want to find a match," Mark insisted.

Finally, Judge Cromer warned SBI officials that he would find them in contempt of court if they did not immediately proceed with the DNA testing. On December 19, they began looking for a match.

When I left Winston-Salem to spend Christmas with Milt's sister in New York, I still didn't know what, if anything, had been found.

On Christmas morning, my sister Rita called. I was at the kitchen table eating breakfast when the phone rang.

"Are you sitting down?" Rita asked.

"Yes," I said.

"It's finally happened, Jo Anne. They released Darryl Hunt yesterday."

* * *

The day after my return home to Winston-Salem, Rita brought me all the newspapers she had saved for me while I was out of town.

The front page of the *Winston-Salem Journal* on Saturday morning, December 20, 2003, featured Darryl's picture at the top of the fold.

The headline stretched across the entire page: "New Suspect in Hunt Case."

"They did a DNA test on him. He is a perfect match," Mark was quoted as saying. "They have the rapist." At that time, even he didn't know the name of the suspect.

The reporter wrote, "it was not immediately clear if the news might lead to freedom for Hunt."

Larry Little was quoted as saying, "Hopefully, everything will come to an end."

But Tom Keith was not ready to acknowledge Darryl's innocence. "We've all known that there's a third person since 1994," he said.

Again the next day, the entire front page of the *Winston-Salem Journal* covered news about Darryl Hunt with the headline, "New Suspect, New Clues."

In the first paragraph, I read, "A man who was picked out of a lineup but was never prosecuted in a downtown rape six months after the murder of Deborah Sykes is the new suspect in that case."

Willard E. Brown, 43, was identified as the man.

In looking for a match, the SBI had hit upon Brown's brother. The match wasn't exact, but it was close enough to warrant a closer look at the rest of his family. They tested Brown, and his DNA matched the evidence in the Sykes' case perfectly.

The article reported that Darryl had first heard the news when he called his wife, April, for his usual Saturday morning chat. "I'm very elated about it," he was quoted as saying in a telephone interview. "My faith is that this is it. My experience with the system in Winston-Salem makes me wonder what they'll try to do next."

What horrified me the most was that police had suspected Brown in the Sykes murder after a second rape in downtown Winston-Salem on February 2, 1985.

The article reported that a 20-year-old woman had parked her car about 8 a.m. on Poplar Street and had walked to her office at Integon (now GMAC), a couple of blocks from where Sykes was attacked. A man with a gun had forced her to her car and ordered her to drive to a drive-in movie theater on Old Greensboro Road where he raped her and stabbed her in the face 12 times. She escaped to an apartment complex nearby.

The victim identified Brown in a lineup but didn't prosecute. There had been no witnesses, and police had warned her that it would have been her word against his. By the time she identified her attacker, Darryl was already in jail. When police checked Brown's prison record to see where he was at the time of the Sykes murder, it showed that he had been in jail.

After Zerwick's series ran in the paper, including information on the Integon rape, police checked Brown's record again and discovered that that he was actually on parole and had been released on June 14, 1984 – a couple of months before the Sykes murder.

I felt even sicker when I read that Mark had tried to connect Darryl's case to the Integon rape but was unable to obtain the name of the victim or the suspect from police. The evidence had been destroyed when the case was deemed closed.

A second front-page article bore the headline "Evidence stirs some angry reactions" and reported that supporters showed emotions that ranged from "guarded elation" to "angry accusations against prosecutors and police."

Rev. Carlton Eversley was quoted as saying, "The hands of the police and prosecution in this case now drip with the blood of Ms. Sykes."

* * *

The typeface of the front-page headline on Christmas Day was the largest I had ever seen. "I always had faith" it quoted Darryl as saying.

"Darryl Hunt walked out of the Forsyth County Jail just before noon yesterday," the first paragraph read.

"It feels great . . . to finally be free and vindicated," he said on the jailhouse steps. "I don't think there's words to express how I feel."

Darryl Hunt was released on an unsecured $250,000 bond, and a hearing was set for February 6.

According to the release order signed by Judge Cromer, Brown confessed on December 22, 2003 to killing Sykes. He said he acted alone.

The article reported that many of Darryl's friends thought he would be released December 23 – at least temporarily – but that Keith had decided he needed more information. He waited until about 5:30 a.m. Christmas Eve to call Mark and arrange to meet him and Judge Cromer at the Forsyth County Hall of Justice later that morning.

Dozens of Darryl's supporters had gathered at Emmanuel Baptist Church the day before, expecting his release and facing another disappointment. State Rep. Larry Womble stood outside with a cell phone in one hand, calling supporters and urging them to meet at the church.

While they waited the next day, the crowd sang an altered version of "We Shall Overcome" using the words, "Darryl has overcome, Darryl has overcome, Darryl has overcome today. Deep in our hearts, we did believe, Darryl would overcome some day."

Just after 1 p.m., Darryl walked out of the jail, hand in hand with his wife, April, and into the arms of some of his supporters, the reporter wrote.

When I read the words, I wept again – with joy that Darryl was free, but also with regret that I hadn't been among the crowd on the day we had all waited so long to see.

*How does someone say they're sorry for
something like this, I wondered.*

CHAPTER EIGHTEEN

On February 6, 2004, Superior Court Judge Anderson Cromer exonerated Darryl Hunt.

As I walked through the rain to the Forsyth County Hall of Justice to attend the hearing, I thought about how different I was from the woman who had made that same walk to testify for Darryl in 1985.

Almost 20 years had given me a few extra pounds and a few more wrinkles, but it had also given me a sense of confidence I could have used when I walked to the witness stand as a terrified 50-year-old.

Part of me wished I could do it all over and perhaps be more convincing in my answers. The other part realized that nothing I could have said differently would have stopped the injustice.

Nobody searched me when I walked in the front door of the courthouse. I told the sheriff's deputy I was there to attend Darryl Hunt's hearing, and he escorted me to a small room to wait.

As I sat there alone, my heart raced. I was glad I had brought one of Milt's handkerchiefs to wipe the beads of perspiration gathering on my upper lip.

After a few minutes, the sheriff's deputy came to the door.

"They're coming," he said, and I could hear what sounded like a party making its way down the hallway.

I stood, anxious to catch my first glimpse of a free Darryl.

The first person I saw was Larry Little, amidst a swirling sea of faces. Somewhere in that crowd is my Darryl, I thought. Larry saw me and turned around and spoke to the person behind him.

"Look who's waiting for you, Darryl," he said.

And at those words, I felt like I was watching the parting of the Red Sea, as a beaming Darryl Hunt broke free of the crowd and walked toward me, his arms outstretched. He towered above the supporters around him, and the room grew quiet as we held each other in a long embrace.

"You always said the day would come when you would be freed, and I believed you," I said. "It's been a long time coming."

Darryl smiled down at me and turned to introduce the woman standing slightly behind him. April Hunt wore a brown suit and her head was covered with a white scarf.

"Ms. North, I want you to meet my wife," he said as though he were offering me his most prized possession.

"I'm so pleased to meet you, Mrs. Hunt," I said and hugged her. Darryl's wife smiled, exposing a flash of gold among her other perfect white teeth. I was struck by how alike she and Darryl looked. Same round face. Same almond-shaped eyes. Same inner glow.

The sheriff's deputy came back into the room to count the number of people who needed seats. I was counted along with Darryl and April and her parents, his lawyers from both trials, Larry Little and several others.

Finally, we all filed out of the room and down the hall in what felt like a victory parade.

Courtroom 5A was small and filled with about 250 to 300 people. The numbers were the same as the first trial, but the crowd was very different. Squeezed into the rows of seats, standing at the back and around the sides of the room, I saw almost as many whites as blacks this time and wondered where they had been 20 years before. I knew that another room held an overflow crowd watching the hearing on closed-circuit television.

Larry Little found a place for me on the front row between April Hunt and her father Imam Griggs. Darryl sat at the defense table in front of us with his lawyers.

Many of the faces in the courtroom looked like a battlefield of warring emotions. Relief that the case was finally over fought with a darker reaction to the fact that an innocent man had spent the better part of his life in prison for a crime he hadn't committed.

How does someone say they're sorry for something like this, I wondered.

As I sat looking at some of the tortured faces around me, I was grateful that I had listened to Dr. Jack Noffsinger's advice and had followed my heart.

"If you don't follow your heart, one day you may be sorry," I remembered him saying.

Winston-Salem had changed since Darryl's first trial. Highway 52 still divided the black section of town from the white, but the division wasn't as wide and the edges weren't as sharp. Students attended the schools of their choice, and we hoped that integrating the younger generation would erase the barriers between the black and white parents and grandparents.

As I looked around at the people in the courtroom, I wondered how many of them had believed he was guilty. I saw a few who had actually played a role in locking Darryl Hunt behind bars for almost 20 years.

District Attorney Tom Keith agreed with Mark's motion to vacate the judgment against Darryl, but he didn't apologize.

Judge Cromer acknowledged that a mistake had been made but didn't apologize either.

"I grant the relief requested by both the defendant and the state to vacate this judgment," he said. "And furthermore with the consent of both parties, we will dismiss this case with prejudice." [9]

Darryl Eugene Hunt would never be tried again for the murder of Deborah Sykes.

As Darryl's eyes swept upward in thanks to the unseen Power to which he had prayed five times a day for so many years, I heard Mark say, "It's all over."

Keith told the judge that Mrs. Jefferson would like to speak. Dressed in a black jacket and a beige turtleneck sweater and slacks, she stood, gripping the side of the witness stand.

"I think what you're about to do today is set free a guilty man who's guilty of my daughter's death," she managed to force through clenched teeth.

Darryl sat straight in his chair with his head slightly bowed. From where I sat, I could see his face. He looked at the grieving mother and did not blink.

After Mrs. Jefferson had returned to her seat, Darryl stood at the defense table. He took a deep breath and bowed his head.

"It's hard for me," he said, stopping to wipe his eyes with a white handkerchief. "Twenty years I've been trying to prove my innocence. Thank you. I give thanks to God and thanks to this court."

Finally, he turned and faced Mrs. Jefferson.

"Mrs. Jefferson," he said, "I had nothing to do with your daughter's death. I wasn't involved. I know it's hard. I just ask that you and your family know that in my heart and my prayers ... that you are in my prayers.

"I feel the pain you felt.... I didn't do it. I wasn't there. I can't explain why people say what they did and why they lied. Only God can."

He didn't blame a soul for the almost 20 years he lost behind bars. Not the district attorneys who worked so hard to present

---

[9] Winston-Salem Journal, February 7, 2006.

the case against him. Not the witnesses who lied and the police investigators who manipulated them. Not the juries who found him guilty and sentenced him to life. Not the judges who refused him a retrial, the governor who refused to make things right or the community who looked the other way.

Instead, he forgave.

Mrs. Jefferson's expression never changed from the hard mask of hatred she had worn for almost 20 years.

As she marched from the courtroom, our eyes met, and I felt as though I had been stabbed with a poison dagger.

As Darryl and April walked out of the courtroom together, hands reached out to touch them. To slap the local hero on the back. To wish him well with his new wife and children. His new life.

I didn't try to fight the crowds. I knew there would be time later for Darryl and me.

*"I want somebody in this community to stand up and
say, 'Darryl Hunt, come to work for me.' That's when
I will know that we have begun to heal." (Jo Anne
North Goetz at a press conference February 6, 2004)*

CHAPTER NINETEEN

Michelle Johnson, a reporter for the *Winston-Salem
Journal,* interviewed me at the press conference at
Emmanuel Baptist Church after the exoneration
hearing. The next day's issue of the paper featured my picture and
comments, along with those of Don Tisdale, Willis Whichard,
the former Supreme Court justice who voted against the third
trial for Darryl, Mayor Allen Joines, Khalid Griggs and Joel Cole,
the only black juror in the two trials.

"I think that we absolutely must close the book on this," I
was quoted as saying. "And we must start the healing process in
Winston-Salem, because it did divide us. We all make mistakes.
Darryl is willing to forgive, and so should the community. I want
somebody in this community to stand up and say, 'Darryl Hunt,
come to work for me.' That's when I will know that we have
begun to heal."

* * *

I drove Darryl Hunt to his first – and only -- job interview.
A member of my church had told me she had heard that
Darryl was being interviewed for a job at the Northwest Piedmont

Council of Governments.   The organization wanted to hire someone to work with ex-cons during their re-entry into society.

Sounded like the ideal job for Darryl – at least to me.

I telephoned him.

"I understand you're interviewing for a job at the Northwest Piedmont Council of Governments," I said.

"Yes, ma'am."

"Would you like me to pick you up and go with you?"

Darryl paused for less than a minute. "Can you be here at 9:30?" I could hear the little boy smile in his voice, and it pleased me to think that he wanted me with him on such an important day. On a day that could possibly be another turning point for him and his new family.

On the morning of the interview, I drove over to the little house on Sprague Street where Darryl, April and her three children lived. I tooted my car horn, and Darryl, wearing a new aqua linen suit, opened the door at the first toot.

I realized I had a rare opportunity that morning – being alone with Darryl – and used it to   talk about something that had been on my mind for some time.

"Darryl, I want to run something by you," I said.

He waited for me to continue.

"For many years, I've been telling your story to my social studies classes. I want to make sure that what I've been saying is correct and that I'm not sharing anything you don't want me to share."

I told him my Darryl Hunt story on our way downtown to Fourth Street.

After I got to the recent happy ending, I looked over at him sitting on the seat beside me.   His head was bowed, but I could see the tear tracks on his cheeks. I reached over and touched his hand.

"That's the story, Ms. North," he said. "But there's another chapter you can add. April and I are going to be married again in a Muslim ceremony. We want you to be there with us."

"I'll be there," I said through my own tears.

When I had heard about the prison wedding ceremony, any joy I felt that Darryl had found a woman to love was dampened by the image of the bars that might separate the two for Darryl's lifetime. Now that he was free, I could truly celebrate with him.

I parked my car a few blocks from the address Darryl had given me and turned off the ignition. I still had a hard time believing I was going to a job interview with Darryl Hunt. Having faith was one thing. Seeing the fruits of that faith was another.

I felt confident that Darryl would get the job. An ex-con working with other ex-cons seemed like an ideal set-up.

"You're going to do fine, Darryl," I said. I knew he was nervous. His left leg had jiggled on the seat next to me all the way downtown. He didn't say a word as we walked the short distance to the door.

A young woman in the front office stood up and came around her desk to greet us.

"Mr. Hunt, it's a pleasure to meet you," she said and then looked at me, eyebrows raised.

"I'm Jo Anne North Goetz, Darryl's teacher," I said. "And friend."

The woman smiled and waited, as though expecting me to say something more.

"I want to thank you for giving him the opportunity to apply for this job," I said.

"We're happy to consider him," she said, evidently satisfied with my purpose for being there. She handed Darryl a job application to complete. "After you finish filling out the form, use the blank space on the back to write a short essay about what you believe you can contribute to the job."

Darryl's expression didn't change. He nodded his head and sat down with the clipboard she had given him to write on.

I wanted to ask Darryl if he needed help but decided against it and moved to a chair in the corner to read a magazine. The lobby was quiet except for the scratching of Darryl's pen as he took his time with each entry. I could hear him hesitate when he got to the essay, but still I didn't interfere.

After about fifteen minutes, the young woman came back into the room where she had left us.

"Are you finished, Mr. Hunt?"

"Yes, ma'am."

"Thanks for coming by. We'll call you."

I was surprised there was no formal interview, but still left feeling good about Darryl's chances. I was proud of the way he had handled himself in every newspaper interview I had read and knew he would be an asset to anybody who hired him.

Walking to the car was like parading down the street with a celebrity. People yelled congratulations to Darryl from all sides, and he always waved and shouted his thanks.

After many stops along the way to chat with well-wishers, we finally made it back to the car, and I drove Darryl home. When we pulled into his driveway, and I turned off the ignition, I told him I had something to give him -- a blue ribbon with the words, "Who I Am Makes a Difference." [10] I told him to put it on his mirror where he could see those words often.

"Who you are *does* make a difference, you know, Darryl."

"Yes, ma'am. I know. You taught me that a long time ago."

* * *

As weeks passed, and I hadn't heard anything from Darryl about his job application, I decided to call him.

"Darryl, have you heard anything about the job?" I asked.

"I didn't get it. They hired somebody with a college degree and more experience. They said it was a problem that I was missing 19 years on my job resume."

---

[10] Jo Anne Goetz is a member of Difference Makers International, a non-profit organization that teaches children and adults how to show their appreciation, respect and love for one another.

I felt as shocked as I had when I first saw his picture in the paper after his arrest. And as awed by his acceptance – the same acceptance I had observed during the past two decades.

I wasn't Darryl Hunt, though. Jo Anne North Goetz wanted to march downtown and demand that they give him the job.

Once again, I followed Darryl's lead and tried to accept – but I had a hard time doing it.

* * *

Milt and I received an engraved invitation to the Hunt wedding. On the front of the card, two hearts with the words "Mu'mina" and "Muhammad" were joined.

Inside was the quote: *And among His signs is this, that He created for you mates from among yourselves, that ye may dwell in tranquility with them, and He has put love and mercy between your hearts: Verily in that are signs for those who reflect. (30:21)*

The invitation appeared on the opposite page.

In the name of Allah the Most Gracious, Most Merciful
The Honor of your presence is requested
at the Nikah (Islamic Wedding Ceremony) of
Muhammad Atiba (Darryl Eugene) Hunt
and
Mu'mina (April Clark) Hunt
On Sunday, October 17, 2004
at
The Community mosque of Winston-Salem
1419 Waughtown Street
at 3:00 p.m.
Attire: Semi Formal
Reception to follow at the Hawthorne Inn
420 High Street

A note was tucked into the invitation informing us that the time had been changed from 3 to 5:30 p.m. so as not to interrupt the Ramadan fasting of the Muslim guests.

Milt and I had never attended a Muslim service and looked forward to our new experience.

* * *

Several weeks later, I met Darryl downtown to deliver my wedding present -- a set of dinnerware.

As I took the gift from my car and transferred it to his truck, I asked him about his plans for the future. Darryl smiled -- in the way only a man who has been to hell and back can -- and told me he was looking forward to being a father to April's three children.

"I'm going to love them like they were my own," he said, and I knew those were not just words. Not just an empty promise. Not just Hallmark card sentimentality. Darryl Hunt might never have biological children of his own, but I knew he had the heart of a father. He had learned how to love, discipline and enjoy a child from one of the finest – his grandfather.

* * *

Milt and I celebrated Darryl's and April's marriage with about 50 of their close friends and family.

As we walked up a long flight of stairs to the front door of the mosque on the wedding day, I marveled at how a little boy raised in the First Baptist Church in East Winston had found his way to this place.

I had never been to a Muslim ceremony, but Darryl had coached me on proper etiquette. We took off our shoes and left them in a vestibule outside the large open room where the service was to be held, and then Milt left me to sit with the men. I found a folding metal chair on the women's side of the room.

After a simple ceremony performed by Imam Khalid Griggs, about 150 other guests joined the wedding party for a reception at the Hawthorne Inn near Old Salem.

Before they left the mosque, Darryl and April changed from their white wedding attire into shimmering gold suits made with fabric they had bought at the Harlem Market near the mosque where Malcolm X had worshipped.

The guest list at the reception looked like a Who's Who of Winston-Salem and included the mayor, several members of the city council and a state representative. Milt and I sat at a table with Mark Rabil and his wife, Judy, and Phoebe Zerwick, the *Winston-Salem Journal* investigative reporter who had written the eight-part series that exposed the injustice of Darryl's case.

As I looked at Darryl Hunt sitting at the long table at the front of the room with his bride, her three children and her parents, I thought about my grandmother and one of her favorite lines. "I feel like I've died and gone to heaven," she always said during her happiest moments.

There was no champagne that day, but the lemonade flowed freely as we toasted the couple.

When it was my turn, I previewed my toast with stories about Darryl emptying the mouse traps and standing up for me with the class bully.

"In the sixth grade, Darryl was my protector," I said, "and when he needed me to return the favor, I was proud to stand up for him.

"It's been a long 20 years, but I never lost faith. Along the way, I have been proud of Darryl as I watched him accept the injustice inflicted on him. And I have been proud as I watched him pray for and forgive the people responsible for that injustice.

"I wasn't sure whether the world would ever be convinced without a doubt that Darryl Hunt didn't kill Deborah Sykes, but I would have gone to my grave believing he was innocent."

EPILOGUE

On April 15, 2004, Gov. Mike Easley pardoned Darryl Hunt, entitling him to receive $20,000 for each year he was wrongly imprisoned, or about $360,000.

The Winston-Salem City Council appointed a citizen's panel (Sykes Administrative Review Committee), which spent more than a year reviewing the investigation into the Sykes murder. In February 2007, a 9,000-page report of their findings was released to the public, showing, among other things, that there is no evidence that Darryl Hunt was involved in the Sykes rape or murder; that for at least two search warrants in the Sykes case, it appears that detectives used false information; that some of the same detectives who worked on the Sykes case also worked on three other similar rape cases in 1984 and 1985 and either failed to consider or failed to document connections between those cases; and that the police failed to turn over to defense attorneys documents that had been prepared for the Sykes case.

In February 2007, Darryl Hunt settled his case against the city and the police officers involved in the case for $1.65 million.

For her support of Darryl Hunt, Jo Anne North Goetz received the Humanitarian Award at the Ministers Conference held in Winston-Salem, North Carolina on January 19, 2004.

In February 2005, Hunt incorporated The Darryl Hunt Project for Freedom and Justice and serves as its executive director. Goetz serves on the board of directors and plans to donate a portion of the proceeds from the sale of this book to its work.

THE DARRYL HUNT PROJECT
FOR FREEDOM AND JUSTICE

The mission of The Darryl Hunt Project for Freedom and Justice is to provide assistance to individuals who have been wrongfully incarcerated. Working closely with the North Carolina Center on Actual Innocence, the Project refers cases for screening and assists with local cases or where the Project has special expertise. At this time, it is only able to assist with a small percentage of requests, but does respond to everyone requesting assistance.

The Project helps ex-offenders obtain the skills, guidance and support they need as they return to life outside the prison system. Re-entering the community after incarceration can be a confusing and frustrating time, particularly when felony convictions create huge barriers to finding jobs and housing. Darryl's commitment is to help ex-offenders, known in the Project as "associates," find jobs and housing during the critical first 90 days after release, in the hope that one conviction doesn't become a life sentence. Re-entry associates have an excellent record of finding and keeping jobs and building stable and productive lives.

The Project also advocates for changes in the justice system so that more innocent people – people like Darryl Hunt – will not spend time in prison for crimes they didn't commit.

Contact Information:

Eight West Third Street
Suite 350
Winston-Salem, NC 27101
Phone: 336-831-1912
Fax: 336-831-1903
Email: darrylhuntproject.org
www.darrylhuntproject.org

ACKNOWLEDGMENTS

by Jo Anne North Goetz

I am grateful to Darryl Hunt for sharing with me his life lesson in faith, forgiveness and patience. Freedom was a long time coming for him and for those of us who waited with him.

I am also grateful to my family. The fear I felt as a witness during Darryl's first trial, and the disappointment and frustration I experienced during his long incarceration, were easier to bear because of their support. Thanks to my mother and father, Maude and Fred Vannoy, my brother, Sonny Vannoy and his wife Joy, my sisters and their husbands, Peggy and Paul Hawkins and Rita and Dennis Taylor and Heather and Sean Busher, their daughter and son-in-law. Their love, support, and understanding of my commitment to Darryl's case were invaluable.

Many others encouraged me along the way, and I would like to thank them, as well.

- My husband and loving partner, Milt Goetz, for his support. Without it, this book could not have been written.

- Betty Love, a true friend, for introducing me to her boss, for her support throughout the years and her willingness to help with this project.

- Tommy and Gwen Andrews, for their love and faith that "We shall overcome."

- Dr. Jack Noffsinger, Pastor Emeritus, Knollwood Baptist Church, for his wise counsel. Without it, I would not have had the courage to take the witness stand during Darryl's first trial in 1985.

- Mark Rabil, defense attorney, for his diligent work, his respect for my role in Darryl's life and for keeping me informed during the long wait.

- April Hunt, for her deep and abiding love for Darryl. Her calm and easy-going manner helped him focus on better days to come. Her love sustained him in his darkest hours.

- Iman Kahlid Griggs, her father, for giving Darryl a home during the months between the first and second trial and for sharing news with me after he returned to prison.

- Phoebe Zerwick, investigative reporter for the *Winston-Salem Journal*, for the research and writing that exposed the facts that led to Darryl's freedom.

- Dr. John Mendez and Dr. Carlton Eversley, two ministers who never let God rest for almost 20 years. Their constant encouragement and support throughout the whole ordeal was awesome. The depth of their commitment is astonishing.

- Judge Andy Cromer, for his fearless belief -- even though he was newly-elected -- that DNA was the answer. My deepest gratitude for his fortitude and perseverance.

- Johnny Totten, attorney in Charlotte, N.C., for his support after the trial. As a fellow member of Knollwood Baptist Church and law clerk working in the Forsyth County court system, he kept me informed about the case after the trial.

- Fred Flagler, Editor, *Winston-Salem Journal* and *Winston-Salem Sentinel* and fellow member of Knollwood Baptist Church, for believing in my dream of Darryl's freedom even in the middle of the nightmare of his co-worker's murder.

- Larry Little, assistant professor of political science at Winston-Salem State University, for his kindness every time I encountered him.

- County Commissioner Walter Marshall and Rep. Larry Womble for publicly defending Darryl's innocent.

- City Councilman Nelson Malloy for his continuous encouragement to Darryl. His commitment was above and beyond the call of duty. His dedication and love helped keep it all together in the midst of all the disappointments.

In an effort to tell my story, I have attended many seminars during the past five years. I would like to thank:

- Helice Bridges, founder of "Who I Am Makes a Difference" and recipient of the Gandhi Award for her acknowledgment of people all over the world. She has truly made a difference for me.

- Jack Canfield, America's Success Coach, is the founder and co-creator of the billion-dollar book brand *Chicken Soup for the Soul* and a leading authority on Peak Performance. He is a former teacher and donates 10 percent of his royalties to charities.

- James Malinchak, College Speaking Success author and motivational speaker, for his advice, "Write a book, you can do it."

- Keith Froehling, Master Yes Experience, for his belief in me and my ability to succeed.

- Debbie Allen and Patricia Noel Drain, co-founders Maximizing Success, for their seminars and the opportunity to meet other speakers.

- James Ray, an expert in the science of success, for his seminars in becoming completely happy with life. A guest on Oprah, he validates "The Secret" by his sharing with others.

Finally, to Leigh Somerville McMillan, the insightful writer of this book, for being with me every step of the way and for her authentic friendship. It was an honor working with her.

As a public speaker, I like to call myself "Queen of SILK" (Serve Individuals Love and Kindness). As you read this book, think about the people who may need your love and kindness – the Darryl Hunts in your own life.

In the words of Catherine Ryan Hyde, "Pay it forward."

Blessings,

Jo Anne North Goetz

ACKNOWLEDGMENTS

by Leigh Somerville McMillan

I met Jo Anne North Goetz while covering an event for my local society column. I was still reeling after my son's four-day kidnapping episode in Haiti and knew I was not at my best that night. Instead of shaking my hand when we were introduced, Jo Anne enveloped me in the kind of hug that helped me forget every mother's worst nightmare – at least for an hour.

A few months later, she called and said she wanted to talk to me about writing a book. I met her for lunch, enjoyed the food and her story but told myself that she was just another person with misguided notions of writing a best seller. I didn't think I'd ever hear from her again.

I was surprised when she called in August and asked me if I was ready to begin writing.

Thank you, Jo Anne, for sharing your story and for believing I could write it.

Thanks to Darryl Hunt and Mark Rabil for their willingness to tell their stories *one more time* and for reading this piece of creative non-fiction to make sure I didn't stray from the shocking truth.

To Tommy Andrews for helping me to envision the jail that was torn down to build a parking deck and Anthony Burnett and Barry Sales for their stories about growing up with Darryl.

Heartfelt thanks to my husband, Jim McMillan, for staying with me throughout the months of obsessive working, for reading each page and offering such valuable legal and literary advice; my dog Mercy, who required necessary breaks from the long days in my studio; my Taos writing group friend, Nancy Jainchill; and my mother, Jerrie Rutledge, who has been reading my work since I was 5 years old and who, even before she read the first word, thought this book was better than anything John Grisham ever wrote.

And to Forsyth County Clerk of Court Terry Holbrook, who gave me access to the first trial transcript; and Nannette Davis for the introductory Kierkegaard quote.

To Phoebe Zerwick for her nine months of digging through more than 30,000 pages of documents and writing the brilliant eight-part series, "Murder, Race, Justice" for the *Winston-Salem Journal*. Without the benefit of her work, I would never have tackled this project.

Finally, to Ricki Stern and Annie Sundberg who spent 10 years working on the documentary, *The Trials of Darryl Hunt*, which allowed me to see and hear the characters about whom I wrote.

About
Jo Anne North Goetz

Jo Anne North Goetz knew she wanted to be a teacher from the time she was offered the opportunity as a third-grader in a one-room schoolhouse in the Appalachian Mountains of North Carolina. She graduated from Appalachian State University in 1956 and enjoyed a teaching career that spanned 42 years and won her induction into the prestigious Rhododendron Society of the Reich College of Education at ASU.

Goetz was employed for 31 years in the Winston-Salem/ Forsyth County school system and for eight years in DeKalb County, Georgia, where she served as the chairperson of the DeKalb County Teacher Forum. She returned to Winston-Salem in 1999 and became a teaching mentor for three years.

She worked for 33 years in the Governor's School of North Carolina at Salem College in Winston-Salem as the Director of Recreational Activities for Academically and Artistically Talented Students. In 2000, she organized and served as chairperson of the Governor's School Foundation.

Goetz's other honors include the 1984 Philo Middle School Teacher of the Year Award and a 1994 DeKalb County School District Junior High School Teacher of the Year Award. In 1996 she received the Order of the Long Leaf Pine from Gov. James B. Hunt, Jr.

Geotz is past president of Retired School Personnel, has held offices in the Winston-Salem Twin City Host Lion's Club and served as a deacon at the Knollwood Baptist Church.

About
Leigh Somerville McMillan

Leigh Somerville McMillan has pursued a lifetime of writing that predates her career as a writer. As a child, she loved stories and was delighted to learn to hold a pencil and capture them on the page. Words have always provided her greatest entertainment, but it was only after she received her English degree from Salem College in 1999 that they began to provide her source of income.

McMillan was the first winner of the Annette Allen Creative Writing Award in 1999 and received a 2003 Journalism Contest Award from the North Carolina Press Association. She was a reporter for the *Business Journal of the Triad* and currently writes a weekly column for the *Winston-Salem Journal* and bimonthly for *Winston-Salem Living Magazine*. She has been published in *Attache* and *Sky* magazines, various corporate trade publications and is the ghost-writer for a long list of memoir clients. McMillan has recently completed her first novel, *Ben*. For more information, visit www.studiomcmillan.com.

Printed in the United States
73654LV00006BA/1-195

9 781434 301703